WHAT PEOPLE ARE SAYING ABOUT *TURNING POINTS* . . .

"The stories shared in this book are powerful examples of how people can survive and be transformed by the unexpected, uncontrollable, and overwhelming situations in their lives. It is through their challenges that they have come to experience life with a real sense of presence, spaciousness, and peace. I highly recommend this book; it will give you what Anne Lamott states as the two best things: 'softness and illumination.'"

—**Mary Weiler, ND Chapter Chair for the American Foundation for Suicide Prevention, mental health advocate**

"This is a book about struggles. About resilience. About second chances. I believe that any person who has been told they are not worthy because of their past experiences should read this book. This is a resource many of us have been waiting for."

—**Reverend Mytch Pierre-Noel Dorvilier, Multi-Ethnic Mission Developer, Eastern North Dakota Synod, ELCA**

"Turning Points is a testament to the human spirit of resilience. It is also a reminder that we are not alone in this often-difficult journey through life. Turning Points can give us hope during these challenging times."

—**Nate Aalgaard, Executive Director, Freedom Resource Center**

TURNING POINTS

*True Stories of Thriving
Through Adversity*

Laetitia Mizero Hellerud

Turning Points
True Stories of Thriving Through Adversity
By Laetitia Mizero Hellerud © 2018

All rights reserved. Use of any part of this publication, whether reproduced, transmitted in any form or by any means, electronic, mechanical, photocopying, recording, or otherwise, or stored in a retrieval system, without the prior consent of the publisher, is an infringement of copyright law and is forbidden.

While the publisher and author have used their best efforts in preparing this book, they make no representations or warranties with respect to the accuracy or completeness of this book and specifically disclaim any implied warranties of merchantability or fitness for a particular purpose. No warranty may be created or extended by sales representatives or written sales materials. The advice and strategies contained herein may not be suitable for your situation. You should consult with a professional where appropriate. Neither the publisher nor the author shall be liable for any loss of profit or any other commercial damages, including but not limited to special, incidental, consequential, or other damages. The stories and interviews in this book are true to the best of the publisher's and the author's knowledge. Names and identifiable information may have been changed to maintain confidentiality.

The publisher and author shall have neither liability nor responsibility to any person or entity with respect to loss, damage, or injury caused or alleged to be caused directly or indirectly by the information contained in this book. The information presented herein is in no way intended as a substitute for counseling or other professional guidance.

Hardcover ISBN: 978-1-7327948-0-1
Softcover ISBN: 978-1-7327948-1-8
eBook ISBN: 978-1-7327948-2-5

Interior and Cover Design by: Fusion Creative Works, FusionCW.com
Author Photos by: Stacy Kennedy Photography

For more information, visit LaetitiaHellerud.com

Published by
UBUNTU Consulting

Printed in the United States of America

To those who are brave enough to choose and find ways to elevate the light instead of being stuck in the darkness. I commend you.

CONTENTS

Why I Wrote This Book	11
Introduction	13
Chapter One: Pushing Through Closed Doors	19
Chapter Two: The Good News	23
Chapter Three: A Full Life	27
Chapter Four: In the Line of Duty	31
Chapter Five: The Healing Power of Recovery	35
Chapter Six: My Son, My Raison d'Être	43
Chapter Seven: The Long Road Toward My Purpose	49
Chapter Eight: Who Needs a Hand?	57
Chapter Nine: Finding Yourself by Giving to Others	63
Chapter Ten: Asking for Help	69
Chapter Eleven: From Survivor to Victor	75
Chapter Twelve: I Am Not Going This Way Alone	81
Chapter Thirteen: Plan B Was My Best Choice	87
Chapter Fourteen: Feeling Powerful and Empowered	93
Chapter Fifteen: Losing My Job and Finding Myself	101
Conclusion	109
Takeaway Messages	113
The Way It Is	116
Acknowledgments	119
About the Author	121

"You can never entirely redeem the experience. You can't make it not hurt anymore. But you can make it beautiful enough so that there is something to balance it in the other scale. And if you understand that word beautiful as not necessarily pretty, then you're getting close to recognizing the integrative power of restoring the balance, which is restoring the truth."

—Richard Hoffman

WHY I WROTE THIS BOOK

"Humans are naturally drawn to the stories of how others cope with loss and adversity because none of us escapes this world without enduring some ourselves."

—Melanie Brooks

We are not powerless. The human ability to self-regulate confers more personal power than you may give yourself credit for. You have the power to control your emotions, your feelings, your actions, and the choices you make every day. You can choose how past experiences impact the rest of your lifetime.

This does not mean that it's easy or swift. What it simply means is that it is *possible*, over time and perhaps with support, professional or otherwise.

Past distresses, even long after the experience, can make you doubt yourself, question life itself, and can rob you of the feeling of being in control. When not successfully processed or effectively resolved,

TURNING POINTS

childhood or past hurts may clutter your present reality. New sufferings may be restimulated as they revive old emotions. How you internalize past hurts and the way you perceive the world around you could also affect your ability or inability to move past emotionally painful circumstances.

My goal in writing this book is to give the contributors a platform to be noticed, to share, or to reclaim their power through the art of storytelling. For the reader, this book is an opportunity to experience our shared humanity as you find yourself in tales from "strangers."

My intention is to inspire you to help you move toward your best future while allowing the contributors to celebrate what they have accomplished over time, through perseverance, and sometimes with support and hard work.

INTRODUCTION

Here is the million-dollar question: How can you ground yourself enough, regardless of where you are or where you have been, so as to be content both for yourself and for the advancement of humankind? Unfortunately, life doesn't come with a manual that you can absorb and simply apply as you sail through it.

Most of us had to go through many trials and errors before figuring out what sustains us on this journey called life. While I am not proposing a recipe for a pain-free life, the stories in this book consistently highlight that a mindset of resilience can be developed by experiencing hardships. Maybe some of the traits the narrators share can be cultivated by anyone seeking to find or enhance their true self.

It might not be obvious, when you are experiencing life's crucibles, that you could emerge on the other side. It's even more difficult to contemplate the possibility that the transformation could be for the better because when in the face of the problem, whatever *it* is, or the pain associated with *it*, your brain may not necessarily register that neither your past nor your present have to be your future.

TURNING POINTS

Some of the stories in this book were not easy to write. Some of the contributors chose to use a pseudonym to protect their identities and preserve the anonymity of their families. While the authors of each of these stories have come to terms with their turning points and have decided to live an authentic life, their relatives might not know what it took for these brave people to get where they are today. Their close circles of friends and family might not be aware of some of the false starts, the emotions attached to those struggles, or the resolutions and what it took to work through them. Out of respect for everyone, names of people and places might have been changed. The good news is that the details that were altered in these stories do not affect their veracity or their powerful message.

The authors recounted their stories generously and candidly because they understand the importance of encouraging others to go after their own passions, to be bold, to be brave, to keep fighting when facing adversity and to lift each other up when you think you have learnt some wisdom. When life becomes unbearable, it's hard not to feel singled out by the challenges, but as Melanie Brooks states in her book *Writing Hard Stories* (Beacon Press, 2017), "The worst story that we can tell ourselves is that we are alone. Human experience is universal though the specifics might vary . . . We find language to unravel the complexities of what happened, and we re-stitch those complexities into narratives that can become meaningful to others. And those are the narratives that have the potential to give others the courage to find their own."

I can think of many times in my own life when I thought it was the end, and I truly felt it. Those are the moments when you have hit rock bottom and you know there is no way to go lower. I am talking about those situations where you are so engulfed with pain and in the confusion, sometimes you forget that you can always consider

INTRODUCTION

the possibility to crawl, to walk on all fours, and in due course stand up again. Looking back at those situations, what I thought to be the end was nothing other than a bend in the journey, where I had no choice but to turn along the path, make adjustments in my plans, take a break to regroup, sit down to regain the strength, restudy the facts, recalibrate the emotions, enroll support, meditate, pray, and embrace the detour.

Depending on the types of challenges I have encountered thus far, whether it was relocating several times as a refugee due to insecurities in my native country of Burundi, losing a parent, being forced to resign from a job I loved, being a single mother for 14 years and raising my children alone in a foreign culture while working multiple jobs and pursuing graduate studies, going through an emotionally excruciating divorce and much more . . . what I found to be the most helpful was to allow myself to feel every single painful emotion associated with each wound—no matter how many of them there were—instead of trying to suppress them or appease them. Those I tried to soothe or numb quickly, I am now learning to relive in order to resolve them properly through proven discharging techniques. Of course, this is harder to do many years later rather than allowing the natural healing process to occur, in stages as needed, immediately following the hurt.

I also learned that once the pain began to subside or when it became more manageable, I would need to map a step-by-step comeback. Each pain and each situation would require a different plan for obvious reasons, but the approach was always the same. I have to say I was not even aware of that process during the periods I applied it. It's only now, many years later, that I can look back and conclude that there was a method. But at the time, I thought I was winging it. I had ways to "measure" or gauge how I was doing or feeling, and

TURNING POINTS

I would build from that space by adding a step I hoped would take me out of the trying situation.

On one of my regular walks with Bruce, a young man I mentor, he recently asked me: "Were you always wise and responsible?"

Bruce made me chuckle a little. No, I wasn't always "wise." However, when I guide my mentees or share advice with a struggling friend today, I speak from my heart about tips that I have tested and that pulled me back up from life's upheavals. Bruce had recently moved out of the family home, was living with one or two roommates, and was struggling to find the right job that paid him well enough to pay all his bills on time. We ended up having a great conversation on this walk and I know he got the answers he needed, even though it's always easier said than implemented. I am aware of that and I made sure to remind him that he has a lifetime to figure out many things. At 19 years old, I thought he was very much ahead of many others his age, looking at what kind of books he reads, who he surrounds himself with, his commitment to learning, and his natural qualities.

As you read the incredibly powerful stories highlighted in this book, you will come to appreciate the many common threads that emerged from anecdotes contributed by complete "strangers" who did not consult with one another whatsoever. The belief in a Creator, a God, or a Higher Power bigger than ourselves is one of the themes. Hard work, the refusal to settle, questioning and challenging the status quo, believing in self, embracing pain, and resolving to find a solution are among the other shared values characterizing the mindset of the authors of these stories.

Not only do the contributors of these stories not know one another, but they also come from different backgrounds, races, professions, sexual orientations, education levels, ages, gender identities, reli-

INTRODUCTION

gions or faiths, socio-economic statuses, and ethnicities, to name a few. I wanted to be as inclusive as possible within the space we had for this book.

What is striking is how interconnected these tales are, highlighting once again how we have more in common than not, as a human species. As the authors of these stories were writing them, I wonder if they could have related to the following thought-provoking words by Edwidge Danticat, a Haitian-American immigrant novelist: "After a while in the process, you have some distance and you start thinking of it as a story . . . Not as *your* story . . . It was a personal grief, but no longer personal . . . [it's] something that has not just happened to me and my family, but something that's happened, in the world."

Realizing and acknowledging that you are not alone in *your* hurt makes it possible to start contemplating and working toward healing. Everyone experiences loss of a loved one at some point in their life; someone else is going through a divorce at this moment; a person you might not know is fighting an addiction or anxiety issues somewhere in the world; and as you read this particular line, at this very moment, a refugee is fleeing persecution somewhere, a transgender person is struggling to be seen for who they are, a gay person is still fighting to love and marry who they choose, a minority family is dealing with racism, oppression, or discrimination, and a young man/woman is being a victim of domestic abuse . . . somewhere. The list is truly endless. As isolated and lonely as it feels when you are besieged by grief and pain, you are not alone. Others, through their individual experiences, do share your pain.

I was driven to compile stories from people who came out on the other side of the sufferings and who were able to look back, and in

TURNING POINTS

hindsight draw lessons to guide others who might be looking for words of encouragement. One thing I have learned is that sometimes something good can come from sad or terrible events.

For those who are genuinely seeking to grow or reignite their hope for life and their faith in humanity, the stories in this book will bring a breath of fresh air, but not until they have exposed some raw brokenness. As much as these stories are about life experiences that force us to reach a point of breaking open, they are also a great testimony to how their authors found ways to elevate the light in the journey instead of remaining stuck in its darkness.

CHAPTER ONE

Pushing Through Closed Doors

"I've always made a total effort, even when the odds seemed entirely against me. I never quit trying; I never felt that I didn't have a chance to win."

—Arnold Daniel Palmer, American professional golfer

First of all, please understand that the story of my struggles is not one of physical or emotional trauma. It is not one of losing my homeland or a loved one. Instead, my story is one of a common, daily ongoing life for a woman, born into privilege, who did not recognize the opportunities that just happened to come to me but were beyond the grasp of nearly all people. I wish I could say that, growing up, I knew in my bones I was privileged, but I think that is an unlikely realization for many of us born white in the middle of a white country.

I was born speaking English in a world where English had become the lingua franca—without obvious disabilities and into a relatively stable family and community. The closed doors were minor and temporary; they were closed, perhaps, but not locked. They were not slammed shut with fury or vengeance or hatred, but because they were not used to being open to women.

I came of age in the 1960s and 1970s, when women were noticing that these doors were beginning to crack open. We had the choice of gently pushing them just slightly on their creaking hinges or slamming them open with shouts of anger and rage. My upbringing, my genes, and my learning brought me to the slower, meeker route of making my way forward. I struggled with questions about worthiness. Was I worthy to enter the man's world? Did I have to let go of being female and all gender identity in order to pursue the life I could see just beyond the horizon?

My first experience of seeing that the doorway of professional opportunity looked different for women than men was my application to medical school in 1975. My college professors and my husband encouraged me to apply. "You are as smart as those young men who think they are so smart!" my physics professor told me. My husband assured me, "I will go wherever you go. I will be with you." But the medical school admissions board did not take well to married women applying to medical school. "What will your husband do?" they asked at the interview. "Where will he go when you have to move around the state for your coursework?" "We need to have committed students who won't just go off and have babies and not practice medicine."

The first time I applied, I didn't get accepted to medical school. I knew the attitudes and comments were discriminatory and "illegal" and yet also knew that if I pursued the pathway of litigation, it would be messy and I probably still wouldn't have the opportunity to explore my dream of medicine. Yet, I didn't see the door as impossibly and permanently locked. There were women in medicine in the state, although not many who were physicians, and most had to choose between marriage and medicine or between motherhood and medicine. But somehow that slight opening was enough for me to slip in and try again.

The following year, I was accepted and began the long process of medical school, residency, and finally the practice of medicine. That time and process showed me the value of perseverance, a humble self-confidence, and trust that the outcome would be the right one, whatever that might look like, even if that meant I would not have a career in medicine because of my gender. By this point, that was okay with me. I also knew, however, that the only barrier to me at the time was my gender. I knew from my upbringing and experiences that I needed to insert myself into an active trajectory of putting my dreams, values, and goals on the line.

There was a sense for me of both actively working toward my goal of practicing medicine and, at the same time, developing an active indifference or acceptance of the eventual outcome. This meant not having an inordinate attachment to a specific understanding of the how, where, and when of my career. Letting go of having to know the details of the journey and the destination was also a gradual process of trusting. It was a gradual letting go of wanting to control what couldn't be completely controlled.

I have looked back at that experience and others similar to it over the years and have added some other insights. I can now see with hindsight and gratitude all of the others who were helping me to make my dreams possible. I can also see the hand of the Holy Spirit silently and gently guiding me all along, though I didn't know it then. These new insights, these new ways of knowing, now give me the confidence that I am not alone. And my membership in the

TURNING POINTS

community of the world means that I, too, must support and guide others in their dreams.

I was fortunate to practice medicine for 30 years. Those professional studies and years of medicine led me into a new direction of guiding. My practices of spiritual direction, leadership development, and teaching are my current ways of giving back the gifts I received. I now walk with others as they ponder their journeys, their struggles and successes, and their relationships in families and communities.

I have had other struggles over the years as wife and mother, and as friend, colleague, and teacher. But I know with a deep abiding certainty that my struggles are nothing compared to the struggles of others who live without the privilege and entitlements that I have known. Because I was born white and English speaking and into a family and community that was not poverty-stricken, I had opportunities that others did not have because of social and cultural barriers. But because my culture was parochial and self-absorbed, socio-centric rather than outward looking, it took a long time for me to learn about oppression and bigotry, racism and abuses related to color and ethnicity. It took a long time for me to learn of humankind's inhumanity toward others who were in some way different.

Today's socioeconomic and political events, nationally and globally, remind me of the work the Spirit calls us to. That those of us born privileged are called to reach out to those who dream of the opportunities we often take for granted. We are called to be less parochial and more global in our vision of what is possible for humankind. I have much to offer and much to learn and that is the way it can be for all of us.

M. J. L., M.D., Ph.D.
Transformational, adaptive, and servant leadership development
Trainer/Coach/Spiritual direction

CHAPTER TWO

The Good News

"So the journey is over and I am back again, richer by much experience and poorer by many exploded convictions, many perished certainties . . . I set out on my travels knowing or thinking I knew, how [people] should live, how [they should] be governed, how educated, what they should believe. I had my views on every activity of life. Now, on my return, I find myself without any of these pleasing certainties . . . When one is traveling, convictions are mislaid as easily as spectacles, but unlike spectacles, they are not easily replaced."

—Quoted in J.S. Wurzel, 2004, *Toward Multiculturalism*

I was born into the Lutheran faith tradition. When my birth mother relinquished me for adoption, she first asked that I be baptized as a Lutheran. Her second request was that I be placed with a Lutheran family, and thus my forever home was selected through Lutheran Welfare Society, which later became known as Lutheran Social Services. My adoptive parents were faithful participants in the

TURNING POINTS

Lutheran church, where I was placed on the Cradle Roll after being baptized for a second time as part of a renewal ritual. My Lutheran pastor uncle and another Lutheran pastor uncle's wife were my baptismal sponsors. I grew up attending Sunday school, soaking up the songs and lessons, and I loved my perfect attendance certificates. I was confirmed in the Lutheran faith and was active in my high school group known as the Luther Leaguers.

I wrote in my diary when I was 12 years old that I wanted to be a missionary and live in a grass hut in Africa. I was challenged in my faith life by the scripture: "Bring the good news to the poor." I didn't understand the ramifications of that mandate, but that calling in my early years continued to mold me as I moved along my faith journey. As time went by, I never lost sight of my desire to "bring the good news to the poor," and I was preparing myself for this in whatever way I could, hoping to someday find how to live it out.

I attended Oak Grove Lutheran High School in Fargo, North Dakota, and went on to the Lutheran Bible Institute in Minneapolis, Minnesota, with the goal of becoming a parish worker in a congregation. Though I felt called to be a Lutheran pastor, this was not an approved call as a woman, so I prayed that I would marry a Lutheran pastor. That prayer was answered, and I became a Lutheran pastor's spouse.

Given my upbringing as a devout Lutheran and despite hearing scripture pretty much every day of my life, no one ever told me that the poor could bring the good news to me. How did my need, my call to be the one tapped to bring the good news to the poor, get so turned upside down?

A simple question during a conversation that took place in a small squatter settlement in Guatemala with people I considered to be the

THE GOOD NEWS

poorest of the poor turned my life in a whole new direction. These people came together as refugees, fleeing the violence of the long civil war in El Salvador. "We read the same Bible you do," a woman in tattered clothing declared with a confident voice. "We also read the mandate to bring the good news to the poor. So the question is, who then are the poor among us?" Those comments, and mostly her question, forced me to take a long and hard look at my life. Certainly, I defined the poor as people who were lacking the material riches the majority of people (myself included) from Western countries surround themselves with. I assumed the poor were those people who were disadvantaged in so many ways, especially those deprived of material resources. I began to realize that the "poor" Jesus was talking about maybe had more to do with spiritual poverty rather than material poverty. I looked into the eyes of the woman challenging me with the question "Who, then, are the poor among us?" and I was suddenly convinced of my own spiritual poverty—and that I needed to relinquish the hold my material wealth had on me.

My life journey took on new purpose in response to that simple question. I'd been reading scripture through the eyes of one who was materially rich, and this quiet but strong believer helped me begin to see with new eyes what the scripture had to say and how important the message of the spiritually rich was for a person like myself, whom I now saw as spiritually poor. I began to hear the words of Jesus in new ways. I began to feel the power of God's Spirit proclaimed through the voices and actions of those free of material wealth. Those who lived the Gospel through their generous spirits, their gifts of true hospitality, and their witness to the One who sustained them daily, even when they did not know where the daily food to feed their children would come from.

TURNING POINTS

I was surprised my Lutheran upbringing hadn't taught me any of this. On the other hand, we were ensconced in the idea that we were the favored ones with all the right answers, and it was we who were called to be the bearers of the good news to the whole world. We had the audacity to believe we were the rich ones and the arrogance to think the poor needed to hear it from us. I was a spiritually poor child and I am so thankful for the woman who challenged me with her question that pierced my soul forever. Since that day, I never talk about the poor without clarifying "materially poor," and continually remind myself and others what I have learned about spiritual richness.

I have learned about humility, compassion, and gratitude while walking the path of my life. I was born into white privilege; I learned this had been a barrier to understanding my true faith and life calling.

Vicki Vogel Schmidt
Co-Founder of Sister Parish, Inc. and
Abriendo Fronteras-Opening Borders/Changemaker

CHAPTER THREE

A Full Life

"The greatest and most important problems of life are all fundamentally insoluble. They can never be solved but only outgrown."

—Carl Gustav Jung, Swiss psychiatrist and psychoanalyst
(July 26, 1875–June 6, 1961)

Life experiences can have many twists and turns, ups and downs, and all can lead to greater personal development. My life excursion has included many changes and opportunities provided by God through key people. My youth was spent in west-central Minnesota. Growing up on a small family farm, the basic disciplines of responsibility and work ethic were thoroughly ingrained in me. Reflecting back on my father, he was a "workaholic," and my mother was very disciplined in religious practice. I have grown to appreciate these traits in myself.

The obvious major turning point in my life was my paralysis, due to a diving accident when I was just short of 19 years old. I could've

TURNING POINTS

easily died but I did not. My God had other plans for my life. My rehabilitation in Fargo as well as in Minneapolis was a big blur, where everyone wore white uniforms and I was removed from my normal element. I began to realize the major change in my life when I was back home nine months later, and my 12-year-old brother was handling the hay bales and chasing the Holsteins. I spent many hours on the driveway of the farm screaming at God and praying, "Why me?"

Fortunately, I had been away from home for one year of college before my paralysis and had some sense of independent life. My vocational rehabilitation counselor recognized my aptitudes and interests and supported my return to college and entrance into an agricultural economics major at a new campus that was wheelchair accessible. It was suggested I should go into social work because I had adjusted so well. Adjusted, hell! I had learned to live with it somewhat.

My college experience was unique. The campus of 2,000 students had 200 people with disabilities and 50 in wheelchairs. We became our own best mentors and friends as we solved common problems. Through sharing our experience with life challenges, we understood what our real potential was—and I began to truly adjust to my new life. My faith experience in college was also different because I heard about, and maybe finally understood, the grace of God. I finally realized my paralysis was not a punishment for some indiscretion.

Another major turning point for independence and a full life experience was driving again and being provided a lift-equipped van that I could drive from my wheelchair. This led to my moving from the farm home to an accessible living facility in Fargo. I hired personal care attendants to help with my basic needs.

A FULL LIFE

The major push in my life at this time was looking for gainful employment. I got some polite interviews and was even offered a job at one time, which was quickly pulled by a supervisor who did not even bother to meet me. While applying for a sales position in 1975, the psychological profile indicated I was not necessarily a salesman and had an orientation to details. This resulted in a job offer as a bookkeeper, working with a lady who had vast experience in cost accounting within a manufacturing operation. This opportunity allowed me to develop more confidence and skills. This job evolved into an office manager position, as well as managing the in-house financing for the structures and products we sold.

My long-term professional goals had been to get involved in finance, and my success resulted in an opportunity to start at the U.S. Small Business Administration in 1980. Here again, I worked with experienced individuals in different areas of agricultural and business finance, which expanded my skills greatly. This federal job resulted in much better pay and greater job opportunities. With the retirement of several individuals, I was able to take advantage of many opportunities to develop professionally.

While living in the accessible housing facility in Fargo, I met my future wife, Sherry, who also has a physical life challenge. We were the only ones in this facility who got out daily for work opportunities and we quickly grew very close. Our relationship developed into a close understanding: we learned that we could provide for each other in unique ways.

Today, we are fulfilled in providing for each other in a balanced, sharing relationship. We've been together for nearly 40 years, and we have developed self-confidence and new skills as we provide for each other's needs. We did not let our physical challenges stop us

TURNING POINTS

from living a full life, including foster parenting and being adoptive parents for our son, Tim.

After my retirement from the SBA in 2010, we became more involved with a nonprofit called Freedom Resource Center for Independent Living. This organization provides mentoring services, information referral, and life-coaching activities to people with disabilities so they can live their lives more fully. We have also been involved as a couple in other community organizations that advocate for accessibility and full inclusion of people with various life challenges. More recently, I have been recruited to be involved in church motivational speaking to help the broader church membership understand people with disabilities and show how our life experience can help other people with situations they encounter. Sherry and I thoroughly believe our life experience was meant to show our community, the church, and other people with life challenges that they can live a broadly fulfilling life.

After the event that left me paralyzed, my turning points were opportunities provided by individuals or experiences that I engaged with and learned from. It is my fervent hope and prayer that other people can learn from my story and see their own potential for a significant, full life experience. This is possible for all people with life challenges, whether they are physical or emotional, and regardless of how serious they are.

Keith Bjornson
Advocate for people living with disabilities/Music lover/Adaptive hunting fan
Freedom Resources Center for Independent Living

CHAPTER FOUR

In the Line of Duty

"Our human compassion binds us the one to the other—not in pity or patronizingly, but as human beings who have learnt how to turn our common suffering into hope for the future."

—Nelson Rolihlahla Mandela, South-African anti-apartheid revolutionary and political leader (July 18, 1918–December 5, 2013)

He had the deepest, darkest eyes. Eyes that took me through a fast-paced tunnel of emotions and led me to his fear. The fear was so deep in his soul, I felt it wrap itself around my heart and lungs, making it hard to breathe.

An everlasting loop of time was imprinted in my memory that day. I remember his face was young, worn, and confused. At 19 years old, I was cocky, strong, and in my mind, invincible. I had to be—I was a U.S. soldier. I'd been in Iraq for 10 months and I knew the drill. We got bombed, we geared up, and we went back to work when the dust settled. I worked beside the locals because they needed jobs and

TURNING POINTS

we needed people to do the unwanted work. That's how I met the grandfather and grandson duo.

The boy's humpback was the first thing that struck me. His spine curved like a force field of protection but also indicated signs of starvation. Barely strong enough to carry his own deformed body, he always assisted his crippled and blind grandfather through the warehouse to their duty post. Out of naivety and curiosity, I would watch the old man beat broken cement pieces with rocks while his humpbacked grandson moved the piles from place to place. A mindless and apparently endless task I had no interest in ever doing.

The sun's heat was so relentless, each ray was a piece of hell thrown by the devil himself. The whistling had started overhead again. BOOM! We all reacted automatically: grab gear and guns, and run. We took off for the bunkers where the duo was working nearby. As we crowded in, I ended up standing so close to the boy and his grandfather that I could smell their presence. Oddly enough, I smelled the same way; everyone smelled awful in that hell heat.

As the rockets rained down around us, my heart started beating so hard that it jolted my body with each pump. The rockets made such a deafening noise that by the third one, the only sounds I could hear were faint voices of those standing right next to me. The rockets were landing so close to us that all I could see through the dust and debris were his eyes and all the emotions they held. In that moment of chaos, I realized the humpback was still a child. A child who had responsibilities that surpassed my own. He lived in an environment where I was counting down the days to leave. In that moment, I realized he would never have that option. As I looked into his eyes, it didn't matter that we came from two different cultures or spoke two different languages. We were sharing the same single emotion:

fear. We both felt that universal emotion as I looked deep into his dark eyes that led me back into my own soul.

When the dust settled and we slowly returned to the work we ran from, I started to breathe again. I don't recall too much from Iraq and when I do, I keep it to myself. A sense of guilt rushes over me every time I wonder about the grandfather and grandson. If I could have laid down my gun in that moment, I would have done it. That day, I realized a bullet will never comfort a broken body, feed a hungry mouth, or heal a broken heart.

Before deployment, we were trained to engage with an enemy—an enemy that was created in my imagination as faceless, rugged, and somehow demonic. The true encounters I had with the people in Iraq were intriguing and piqued my curiosity. If this incident had never happened, I do not believe I would be as passionate about people as I am today. I went to Iraq with a false sense of strength. I left Iraq young, worn, and compassionate.

I don't share much from my experience in the military; it creates a lot of mixed emotions that I never know where to place. I look back at my youth and realize how uncommon my encounter with the grandfather and grandson duo truly was. I have gained much perspective now that I am older, but I recognize the tragedy that it had to come from.

Brandi Nicole Jude
Founder of Invisible Innocence Project/Fearless/Outdoors lover
InvisibleInnocence.org

CHAPTER FIVE

The Healing Power of Recovery

"Recovery is an ongoing process, for both the addict and his or her family. In recovery there is hope. And hope is a wonderful thing."

—Dean Dauphinais, American recovery advocate, writer

I grew up in North Dakota. I have eight siblings, including one who passed away by suicide when I was a preteen. My dad moved out when I was in third grade and I blamed my mom for it. (Don't all kids blame their moms for everything?) The first time I ran away from home I was in fourth grade. I left with two friends who were in my class. Eventually, I returned home that night because one friend's grandma, whose house we had stopped at because we were tired, cold, and hungry, convinced us to call our parents. I had many verbal and physical altercations with my stepdad over time and my relationship with Mom wasn't good either. I was placed in many foster care homes. Some foster homes were good, and some were what nightmares are made of. From one experience in a foster home, I can now say I am a survivor of torture.

TURNING POINTS

Looking back at the extent of the mistreatments I suffered, there is no type of abuse I have not endured from the hands of those many foster parents. Emotional, sexual, and physical—I lived through them all. Still, my spirit was not broken. Someone found the journal that contained my deepest secrets and left threatening notes in it. I freaked out and my reactions landed me in a mental health facility, which ended up being paradise compared to that foster home. I was safe, at least. Over Christmas and for several weeks to follow, I stayed at this facility, convinced that no one wanted me.

I finally was able to go to my dad's and shortly after, I got my own place at the age of 15. I completed alternative schooling so I could work and still graduate with my class. At night, as I laid in my bed, my mind would always go back to the terrible things that happened in my life. I tried to focus on my dreams—dreams about how I would fall in love, get married, have kids, and never let any harm fall on those I loved. When I was growing up, I wasn't protected; I felt thrown away. I felt I wasn't wanted by anyone. I would wonder: Am I a bad person? Did I do something to deserve this? What's wrong with me? For the next 15 years, I would ask myself those questions often, and I struggled to find the ever-elusive, unconditional love I was seeking.

I married at 18 and became a mother to three children. My eldest daughter was born when I was 20 years old. The moment she was born, I found my purpose: to be the best mother to my children that I could be. I realized what it was like to love someone more than anything and know that I would do anything to protect them. I was ready to live happily ever after, but my happily ever after was not to happen . . . yet. The marriage I dreamed of as a child began falling apart before my very eyes. Even though I was miserable in my marriage, it was all I really knew. I was used to the insanity and I was scared to live without any chaos.

I finally walked away. I loaded my two daughters and baby boy in my vehicle and left my children's father. I had no idea how to live on my own, and I was 30! I was very much sheltered in my marriage and not always in a positive way. I wasn't confident in my skin making adult decisions. What 30-year-old doesn't know how to live on their own?! As the divorce proceeded, I realized I was losing everything, right down to the kitchen utensils. I told my attorney to let my soon-to-be ex-husband have it all. I would just keep my children with me. However, that also wasn't happening. The final blow was hearing the judge order that the children needed to go back to their father's home, three hours away from me. The judge placed the kids in my ex's custody.

As the words came out of the judge's mouth, I remember feeling as if everything suddenly moved in slow motion. I remember thinking: I am not hearing her right . . . the court wouldn't take the kids from me! I'm a good mom . . . that's the one thing I am good at . . . this can't be happening! I remember the warmth of my attorney's hand on my wrist and her supporting my back, helping me walk out of the courtroom. I walked out of the courtroom, watching my ex-husband laughing and hugging. A million things were racing through my head: What do I say to the kids? Everything was spinning out of control. I can't do this! I couldn't feel my feet as I walked out the courthouse. I felt as though I floated out of the courthouse to the car. How else would I have gotten there? I don't remember walking or feeling the pavement underneath my feet.

As I climbed into the back of my sister's car, I started screaming . . . screaming at the top of my lungs. It was a sound of death. If death

TURNING POINTS

has a sound, I imagine it to be as extreme as the intensity of my wailing and my sobs. I don't think I had ever heard myself scream like that before. And as those screams were coming out of me, I felt like my spirit had finally been broken. The hope that I held for so many years, hope for someone to love me for who I was, hope for my children to have all they needed, hope to save my marriage, hope to feel peace in my heart, hope for a brighter future . . . all that was crushed and gone, in that very instant. I sat and cried for hours in the back of that car. My mom and others did their best to comfort me while trying to get me inside the house. I could not move. I was frozen in pain and, to various extents, I stayed in that emotional state for the next five years. It was a constant ache. I yearned for death to find me, because I was not worth the grime on the bottom of a shoe. I had lost my purpose the moment I lost my babies.

During those five years, I drank away every emotion that could possibly be felt. If the booze wouldn't work, I would layer it with drugs. I couldn't hold a job. I started pawning what I owned to buy alcohol to hold off the withdrawals from my addiction. My withdrawals got extreme and I would, at times, experience seizures and other adverse effects from the drinking . . . or lack thereof. I ended up homeless for roughly a year. If I couldn't bunk in with someone I knew, I stayed with those I didn't know. Some were safe places, and some were not.

If I had just accepted what was given to me as a child, as a spouse, as an adult . . . or as an alcoholic and an addict—if I had just given in to my so-called fate—*where would I be today*? I would most likely be dead. But as God would have it, He placed an old friend in my path. This man would become my best friend and then, my husband. I finally found that ever-elusive unconditional love I had been looking for. But I had to go through even more bumps before reaching the proverbial "happily ever after."

During our engagement, I was still drinking daily, 24/7. If, at any moment, I didn't drink the amount my body was used to, I would become violently ill. During one of my hospital stays after having a seizure, I opened my eyes to my fiancé crying next to my hospital bed. Part Dutch and German, he is not an emotional fella. He is a big, tall, bald, leather-wearing, stereotypical biker. Through his tears he said, "Babe I can't lose you. We need to do something. I need you in my life." He was so sincerely worried about me and at that moment, I knew I needed help.

We had a wedding date set for May 17th, 2013, but the day I left the hospital we went to the courthouse, grabbed a stranger off the street to be a witness, and tied the knot on January 31, 2013. I was able to go to treatment a week later. I wish I could say that I never drank again, but I cannot. I had bouts of sobriety and then I would relapse. The final time I relapsed, I was coming off of booze at home (something I don't recommend), and I remember having such terrible withdrawal symptoms that I thought I was going to die. I was begging God to forgive all the times I had turned my back on Him, and help me stay alive. "I want to be a mom to my kids. I haven't done what I am supposed to do yet on this planet, please. I don't know how much more my body can handle and I can't do this by myself. I need you, Lord." That was my prayer and my plea.

God did not take my withdrawals away that day, but I did receive an unexpected internal peace alongside the pain. I knew that I was going to survive. I was going to wake up the next day and I was going to live and have another chance at this thing called life. Since that fateful day in August 2014, I have not had a drop of alcohol. I finally put the plug in the jug.

Today, I am a woman living in long-term recovery. I co-parent with my children's father. We go to family functions and sporting events together. We talk to each other often and are always respectful. I am no longer a weekend mom—I am a full-time mom. My daughter, Taylor, moved in with me and my husband over a year and a half ago. She is excelling in school and even taking some college courses. I was able to help my oldest daughter, Jade, move into her college dorm along with the help of her dad and stepmom. No one would believe us if we told them we used to have a police officer present each time we needed to exchange children, because it was that toxic. Thanks to our ability to ask for forgiveness and to extend forgiveness to one another, we co-parent impeccably. My youngest son, Sean, is turning 16 this summer and is such a gentle soul. He takes me out on mom/son dates and has a heart of gold. I can finally be the mom my kids deserve.

A moment I will never forget is when my oldest daughter was speaking at an event and said words I thought I would never hear from any child of mine. She said that the most positive role model in her life was her mom. This was so humbling. I owe that kind of honor to my Higher Power and the healing power that recovery offers those who seek it. When I first got into recovery, my initial sponsor for a 12-step recovery program asked me to write down some goals. I am slowly accomplishing each one of them. I started my own coaching and consulting business and have dedicated my life to helping others find the inner strength to realize their own goals. At almost 40, I am going back to college. I realized it's never too late to start something new. My goal is to be an addiction counselor. Other goals I have checked off include skydiving and bicycling for

THE HEALING POWER OF RECOVERY

a week around the state of Wisconsin. I also recently bought myself a motorcycle and got my passport, and I soon will travel out of the country for the first time.

When people ask me why I have some of these goals, my answer is simple: I am alive! After being comatose for several years, I am going to live a full, exciting, love-filled life because I have been given a second chance to do so. My life is good. It is very peaceful, filled with love from my beautifully blended family of six kids, two sons-in-law, a beautiful granddaughter, and last, but certainly not least, a husband who loved me through it all. I am not saying my life is perfect, but I face stressful situations head-on with optimism and a mindset to find a solution.

I do not regret my past. I have been able to grow through it and learn from it. I can share my story of strength and hope with others. I hope that they, too, will experience a powerful positive change in their lives. Without my past, I would not have the family, friends, career, and life I have now. Damn it, I love my life and I can honestly say I love myself, too.

If you are alive and breathing, you can rewrite your own story. You can make your dreams a reality—it is never too late. Listen to your heart and your soul and live your dreams. We are all worth it and we all deserve peace, love, and happiness. Recovery is possible.

Kerry Ann Leno
Recovery consultant/Motorcycle enthusiast/Dreamer
LenoLeads.com

CHAPTER SIX

My Son, My Raison d'Être

"Being a mother is learning about the strengths you didn't know you had and the fears you didn't know existed."

—Linda Wooten, author of *A Mother's Thoughts*

Joining the military as a 20-year-old was one of the biggest blessings in my life. Being far away from all my family and friends and everything I had ever known made me grow up and mature faster than most of my peers. I learned survival, perseverance, self-worth, self-sacrifice, independence, and interdependence. Life in the U.S. military was a great opportunity for me to develop great friendships, many of which I still have today, five years after being honorably discharged for health concerns. I was able to create lifelong, incredible memories while serving my country.

Unfortunately, my experiences in the military were not all positive and rosy. Some of my worst life turbulences happened while I was serving in the U.S. Air Force. One of those unforgettable

TURNING POINTS

nightmares involved being raped. I remember being at a private party with people I knew and others I had met for the first time. Most of them were fellow service men and women. We were having fun, dancing, eating, and probably drinking more than we should have. The drinks were made and mixed in a separate area away from the lounge where the private party was occurring. I don't remember how the party ended or how I got home. Could it have been that my drink was spiked with drugs? But why would that happen?

The next morning, I could see physical signs that I had been raped. Because I had zero recollection of anything connected to any sexual encounter, I had no choice but to gather my courage and ask one of my friends who was at the party, as well. I needed to know whether they had seen any "weird" situations involving me. I didn't know how to ask the question. They knew exactly what I was saying, and they confirmed my worse suspicion. I had been raped. As we talked, certain details started coming back to my memory. I will spare you those excruciating moments.

The following days and months were strikingly painful as I went through all kinds of emotions ranging from shame—insurmountable shame—to anger and fear. I was frightened that I could have been impregnated or had contracted STDs. I was also scared that if I had, indeed, been drugged and if I had traces of the chemicals in my blood, I could fail the random drug tests routinely done in the military, which could cost me my career. In addition, I was very troubled by the fact that the perpetrator could find me and harm me again. I felt extremely vulnerable. Needless to say, I found myself overthinking all the steps that led to this act. The tape played in my head over and over again and I was miserable.

MY SON, MY RAISON D'ÊTRE

Reports were filed, investigations conducted, and all due processes followed. Eventually an agreement was reached on paper and the case was closed. This, however, as you can imagine, did not mean that I could just move on. On many occasions, I was blamed for this horrific experience. That was stunning! As a victim, I never thought people would find ways to tell me it was my fault. I take full responsibility for the partying that was excessive to some extent. Maybe I shouldn't have hung out with people I had just met or mix that with alcohol. But I certainly did nothing to deserve the sexual assault. I did not ask for it, as some people tried to make me believe.

Even though I did not believe these people, in my head I would ask myself, "What if they were right?" "What if it was truly all my fault?" That self-doubt, the embarrassment, the pain, the hopelessness drove me to severe anxiety and then depression. The mere idea of leaving my apartment to go run an errand sent me into panic-attack mode and for a long time, I did not want to leave my home. Going to work and being around people became a daily chore. I couldn't sleep at night and was feeling lethargic during the day due to the accumulated fatigue. Overall, I was feeling so much guilt and sadness that I didn't know how or if I would ever be able to recover from this nauseating and gruesome experience.

I found comfort in prescription drugs and alcohol. On any given day, I would get drunk and most of the time pass out, so I wouldn't have to feel any longer. But the horrible and powerful memories would haunt me even in my dreams. Going to bed became a new source of anxiety. My life became a living hell. I even thought about ending my life. It seemed like such an act would be better for everyone, my family and friends included. I wasn't even sure if I had faith in God at this point, when I was questioning almost everything about myself and my entire life.

TURNING POINTS

It took me years of processing, professional counseling, medicating, and support, mostly from a handful of friends, before I could function again. I was grateful to have a good health insurance program to take care of my many psychological counseling sessions and the medication I needed for anxiety and depression. By the time I was honorably discharged for PTSD (post-traumatic syndrome disorder) from the military, I was feeling better and excited about the new chapter of my life.

Although transitioning back into civilian life was not as smooth as one would expect, it didn't take me long to get used to it. As I made new friends, I also started dating. I fell head over heels when I met the handsome man I ended up moving in with shortly after. I am not sure if this was a good idea, but Max and I were expecting our first child together only three months after we started living together. This was the happiest I had been in a very long time. Max was so loving and caring. We were both working and thriving in this beautiful home we had purchased together. Although Max was mostly a quiet person who didn't say much, he seemed to enjoy our relationship as much as I did. I felt safe in his presence and was very excited about the future with the son we were expecting.

Unfortunately, my dreams came crashing down on me one day when Max decided to walk away from the relationship without much of an explanation, soon after our son was born and real life kicked in. I was not the fun girlfriend who was always available anymore, now that there was a tiny human being who needed more care and protection and attention than Max did. Looking back, I also know that I had challenges with trust and intimacy, mostly because of the assault I had experienced prior to this relationship. Once again, I found myself overwhelmed with the situation and unable to make sense of what had happened. I tried to find him to get some type of explanation, but to no avail. Family responsibilities were too much to handle alone. I couldn't keep up with the bills and found myself eventually with no other choice but to sell the house and move in temporarily with a relative. I also started to experience postpartum depression. I relapsed back to the only way I knew when dealing with pain: alcohol and prescription drugs for anxiety and depression.

My turning point occurred when I almost overdosed on alcohol and medication. The pain had been too much, and I wanted to end it all. That night, I took enough of these substances to make me violently ill, but (luckily) not enough to kill me, although that was my intention. As I was lying on the floor waiting for this never-ending pain to be over, I was also experiencing excruciating stomach pain. I was trying to drag myself to the bathroom, feeling the urge to throw up. I don't know how long this agony lasted. At some point, I truly felt that I had to be close to dying. I had nothing to compare it to, but the pain, both physical and emotional, was so raw and so surreal that I thought it had to be *it:* death. From nowhere, I heard a very faint voice of a crying baby. My four-month-old son needed his mom. That very instant turned my insane life upside down and for the best.

Up until that cry, motherhood had not totally sunk in. All the times prior to that moment, everything had been about me, myself, and I. For some reason, I wanted to be the center of all attention and I managed to do that mostly in a negative way, through my life choices. But when my son cried, it was almost like I was overcome by some sort of super power and something about my responsibilities toward that little man really clicked. He was crying for help and I was the only one he had. What he didn't know was that I also was crying for help in my sick way. It turned out that he was all I had to save me from my insanity and self-absorption. In all my physical

TURNING POINTS

weakness, I picked myself up, dragged myself to where my infant child was lying, and I laid by his side to comfort him. That ended up being a really long night, but by the morning I was not as nauseous, although still extremely hungover. As I nursed myself back to wellness while tending to my son's needs, I had to make a serious decision right there and then. It became crystal clear that my obligations toward this child were more than enough for me to start looking for help and getting better. My life slowly shifted to embrace this new role fully and all my attention started turning toward my beautiful, innocent child.

Eventually, I started to rebuild my life by moving back to a town closer to family, surrounding myself with supportive people, finding a job, and getting professional counseling again. Almost four years later, looking back, I am convinced that my son saved my life. I have purchased another beautiful home and I recently enrolled in an online program that will, hopefully, help me start a new career when I graduate. Almost all my new friends are mothers themselves and my new ways of having fun are centered around family activities. I love everything about my new life and I celebrate every day that I get to enjoy as a mother.

Martina W.H.
Grateful stay-at-home mom/World traveler/Friend

CHAPTER SEVEN

The Long Road Toward My Purpose

"There are two primary choices in life; to accept conditions as they exist, or accept the responsibility for changing them."

—**Denis Waitley, American motivational speaker, writer, and consultant**

In my short 30-some years of life, I have had many turning points that led me to where I am today. Some were extremely challenging and some were enlightening.

As cliché as this sounds, I truly believe we are never given more than we can handle. During some of the worst points in my life, where I thought I wouldn't be able to get past whatever was going on, I would remind myself that I *can* get through it. I also believe that each of my turning points helped to prepare me for the next challenge. Over the years, I learned I wasn't alone in this journey called life, and each time, I found a support system and a way to keep going.

TURNING POINTS

My first real test was at the age of 17, at the end of the school year. I decided to have an elective breast reduction surgery to lessen back and shoulder problems. I remember my doctor reassuring me there was only a two percent chance that anything could go wrong and that I was safe. Later, those numbers became meaningless for me, as I dealt with life-threatening complications. Those in the two percent category can still die.

The surgery went well, and I was able to go home that same day. A few days after the surgery, I began to feel that something was terribly wrong. Lying in my bed, I was freezing cold and dizzy, and yet I was sweating uncontrollably. I tried to ignore it and rest but I couldn't sleep. I tried to get up, but it was difficult and too painful to move. I was literally stuck in my bed.

I tried calling for my parents, but they couldn't hear me from my basement room. I even attempted using my cell phone to call the house phone and my mom's cell phone. No one answered.

By this point, I was coming in and out of consciousness. Desperate, I called my boyfriend at the time, who lived out of town. Luckily, the call went through and he also tried unsuccessfully to get through to my mother. Again, though, there was no answer.

At this point, I knew I had to help myself. I don't know how I managed to walk a few steps before collapsing in the hallway. My brother heard the noise and came to see what was going on. After that, I am not sure what happened; everything was a blur. I know my parents had me taken to the hospital.

I had a fever of over 106. The doctors were worried my organs would start failing if my fever didn't go down. I could go into a coma or even die. After three days in the hospital, I was more awake and I remember talking with one doctor. He told me I was lucky to be alive. If I hadn't gotten out of bed when I did, I probably wouldn't be here today.

Hearing my doctor tell me I could have died scared me to my core. When we are young, we often assume nothing will happen, that we are almost invincible. I was young and had a full life ahead of me. Hearing my doctor tell me I could have died was a major turning point in my life.

I remember breaking down and crying because I was so grateful to be alive. I had a surgical site infection that turned into a condition known as MRSA (methicillin-resistant Staphylococcus aureus), which is an antibiotic-resistant strain of bacteria. Back then, as now, it is very difficult to heal.

The treatments were intense. I hated the constant blood draws and medication. The strong antibiotics produced a burning sensation when they were administered. It got to the point that when the nurse came in with the I.V. bag of meds, I would start crying because I knew how painful it was going to be.

For weeks, I was alone most of the time except for my parents' lunchtime visits. My friends were working or on vacation. I was especially thankful for my boyfriend at the time, who would commute after work to come and stay with me overnight. He slept in an uncomfortable makeshift hospital bed without complaining.

Prior to my hospitalization, I had scheduled to take the ACT test. Since I was still in the hospital at test time, I had to convince my doctors to let me go take the test. They put in a PICC (peripherally inserted central catheter) line so I would be able to leave, take the

TURNING POINTS

test, and still get the medication I needed. I was hooked up to a small machine that injected medication 24/7.

This treatment only lasted for about two days because my body started to reject the PICC line and I developed blood clots in my arm. I was once again rushed to the hospital where the doctors were concerned the blood clots would cause a heart attack. Again, I was terrified. I hadn't yet recovered from the idea that I had nearly died, but now they were telling me I could have a heart attack. Instead of being admitted back into the hospital, I was sent home with blood thinners and an inserted port, but had to come in every six hours for infusions. I spent so much time in and out of the hospital that at one point I had my own room down by the emergency room. The daily shots of blood thinners in my stomach left horrible purple bruises that were tender to the touch.

It took a good chunk of that summer before my senior year to fully recover. I ended up breaking things off with my boyfriend, mostly because I realized nothing was guaranteed, including tomorrow. I felt like I needed to experience more of life. I was in a constant state of anxiety about petty things and yet I embarked on risky behaviors, almost in a rebellious way. I couldn't deal with my feelings of anxiety.

During my senior year, I felt as if I had become a different person. I wasn't shy or reserved anymore. I was no longer focused on getting good grades or being on the honor roll. I wasn't thinking about college; I just wanted adventure and to try new things. I just wanted to live life. As I look back on the choices I made, I am embarrassed, shocked, and ashamed. I regret a lot of the things I did.

Toward the end of my senior year, I had another turning point in my life. I remember waking up hungover from a party. I didn't know how I got home. After talking with friends at school that morning,

THE LONG ROAD TOWARD MY PURPOSE

they reminded me that I drove myself home. I have no recollection whatsoever of driving that night—but I know I shouldn't have been behind the wheel.

That was my wake-up call to the fact that I was taking my second chance at life for granted. I could have easily died the summer before and here I was, risking my life again—and also other people's lives. I quit hanging out with certain people who I knew were a bad influence. I stopped the drug use and the partying. I started to refocus on my academics. I still wanted to go to college and make something of myself. I finished high school on the B honor roll and was accepted into a couple of colleges.

A few years later, another turning point happened right after turning 21, as a junior in college. I had great ambitions; I was going to double major, then get a master's degree and eventually a Ph.D. I also wanted to make the dean's list every semester, be on the college cheerleading team, and financially support myself. I was in the process of accomplishing all those goals. Then I discovered that my boyfriend of the last three years had cheated on me. When I found out what was happening and confronted him, he left me for the other girl.

A few weeks later, I found out I was pregnant with his child. I was torn and didn't know what to do. I considered all my options and eventually decided to tell him I was pregnant, and that I was planning on keeping the child regardless of his decision. I wasn't going to let my pregnancy prevent me from being on the cheerleading team and accomplishing the goals I had set for myself.

At first, he said it wasn't his baby. At that time, he was dating someone else. Eventually he broke up with the new girlfriend and came back to me just before my son was born.

TURNING POINTS

At 21 weeks, I went into early labor. I was put on strict bed rest for months so I could carry my son for as long as possible. My professors were amazing and willing to work with me while I was out of school. I was scared; I didn't want anything to happen to my baby. While on bedrest and dealing with these fears, I became depressed and started to eat to cope with my emotions. I gained 65 pounds in those two months. My inactivity and stress eating felt awful. My son was born a month early with a few complications but nothing major.

His dad and I moved with our son into an apartment. I had worked in many childcare settings with infants and I knew my son wasn't a typical baby. He was very colicky and would scream and cry, but he didn't want to be held for comfort. As he grew older, he had bizarre triggers or quirks. When he was nine months old, he and I moved out of the apartment as I separated from his dad. Now a senior in college, with about a year and a half left to finish, I became a single mom. I was working three jobs so I could afford daycare and other bills while I went to school full time.

I was so thankful for my parents, who helped take care of my son while I was working on the weekends and evenings. Raising a child on my own, working, and going to school full time were exhausting. There were many nights when I was studying, and I would be in tears. Life was so hard, and I wanted to give up. I ended up dropping some classes because it was becoming too much to handle. My year and a half left started to look more like two years or more before I could graduate.

I was bound and determined to finish college and go to graduate school . . . and I wasn't going to let my life get in the way. I finally got a break when my son got into an Early Head Start preschool program at the age of two. I was able to quit a couple of my jobs

THE LONG ROAD TOWARD MY PURPOSE

since I didn't have to worry about daycare expenses anymore. I could finally focus on finishing school.

My son's preschool teachers began noticing his quirks and brought up the things they were seeing daily. They questioned if he was on the autism spectrum because he showed a lot of the typical mannerisms.

I knew he wasn't autistic but there was something about him that was different. My son was very challenging. Getting him dressed was like WrestleMania every morning. I would work up a sweat trying to get him into a car seat and buckled. Dealing with his outbursts was hard and emotionally taxing. For example, I would be dodging flying shoes and toys he threw at me as I drove, while listening to blood-curdling screams. If we went anywhere and he needed to use a public toilet, an automatic flushing system or electric hand dryers would trigger a meltdown and crying that would be hard to control. He hated having his socks off. His shoes had to be tight and if they were not tight enough he would scream, cry, and throw his shoes altogether. He would repeat everything multiple times, over and over again. He would constantly line up everything in a certain order. The Early Head Start staff and I also noticed that my son would only eat certain foods. He hated being touched and would continuously cover his ears to block out noises.

Eventually we had him tested and he was diagnosed with sensory processing disorder. His behavior started to make sense. As challenging as raising a child like my son was, I am thankful for it. He helped me grow into a patient, understanding, and caring person. I ended up graduating with a double major and a minor and was accepted into a graduate school program. It took me two years to finish my graduate studies. I am proud to say that I graduated with close to a 4.0 GPA, despite all the challenges.

TURNING POINTS

I am thankful for the things that happened in my life because without them, I would not be the person I am today. I am now a licensed counselor working in a school. My dream job! I've been told I have "the patience of a saint" when it comes to working with children. I credit my son and his many meltdowns over the years. In addition, growing up with foster siblings for much of my life, I tolerate more than most and understand what kids may be going through. The challenges and obstacles in our lives are there for a reason: to make us better and stronger. They help us become more resilient versions of ourselves.

B.S.G.
Licensed counselor/Child at heart/Fighter

CHAPTER EIGHT

Who Needs a Hand?

"To be yourself in a world that is constantly trying to make you something else, is the greatest accomplishment."

—Ralph Waldo Emerson, American essayist, lecturer, philosopher, and poet (May 25, 1803–April 27, 1882)

When I was born, doctors advised my parents that without my limbs, I would never sit up or walk. During my mother's pregnancy, ultrasounds were not common, so my disability was a complete surprise. Given the fact that my parents were not prepared to have a child with a disability, doctors advised them to give me up for adoption. Luckily for me, they didn't. I don't know much more than that about the story; it is too hard for my mum to talk about it, and my dad is no longer with us.

Embracing the moment and disrupting the norm started the day my parents decided to keep me. Some of the ways this occurred included the first day I defied the odds and sat up, when I stood, and again when I fed myself. Successful people are not status quo. I certainly am not status quo. Successful people all have one thing in common—they are continually innovating and disrupting the norm. For me, innovating and disrupting the norm are just my way of living, breathing, and walking.

My earliest memory was going to kindergarten with all my friends. I grew up in Scarborough, Ontario, in Canada, on a great street called Coxworth Crescent. Scarborough was a bit of a tough neighborhood. Yet Coxworth was a safe haven. Many people on the street happened to be originally from the United Kingdom—Mum is from Liverpool, England, and my dad was from Germany. All our Easter and Christmas holidays were spent house-hopping. People took the Sunday school bus to church together. We were like family. Forty-five years later, we are all still like family. Coxworth was a crescent so there was no through traffic, and only people who lived there came down the street.

As a result, all the kids hung out on the street, played street hockey, had bicycle parades, and played tag and hide and seek, while our parents sat on their front porches watching us and chatting. Because we were all roughly the same age, we were all going to kindergarten at the same time. I had an unwavering belief that we were all going to go to the same school together at the end of the summer, just as the older brothers and sisters had before us. However, come enrollment time, I learned that the local education system told my mum that I needed to go to a "special school." I hate that expression, by the way . . . "special school" . . . "special needs." While writing this, I may have just had a lightbulb moment of understanding about where my distaste for the word "special" comes from.

WHO NEEDS A HAND?

They said the kindergarten teacher could not manage having me in the class. In disbelief, my mum asked *why*. They told her I had to be able to tie my own shoelaces, be able to work my zippers by myself, go to the bathroom, be independent at recess time, and not hold the class up.

Now, it makes sense, actually. These were fairly standard requirements expected of children as they enter kindergarten, and most people assume that without hands, many of these things could not be done. As a teacher myself, many years later, I acknowledge how difficult it would be to manage my needs alongside those of my peers (we were 30 in the class), especially as there was no such thing as classroom aides or educational assistants or "paraprofessionals" back then. As you can imagine, my mum was passionate in her argument to get me in and vehemently explained that I could do all those things. She also explained that all my friends from the neighborhood were going to this school and I was really looking forward to it. Up until then, just like me, Mum had assumed I would automatically be included in our neighborhood kindergarten. Unfortunately, it didn't matter what my mum said; they wouldn't have it.

They had decided without even asking what I was capable of, and the school registrar denied my enrollment. Mum and Dad toured the "special school" and realized quickly that it wasn't the place for me.

We all are faced with "no" in our lives. I get "no" every day as a starting point to most of my requests when the people I am interacting with are approaching me as a four-way amputee. Looking back at how my mum handled my kindergarten enrollment situation, she taught me a valuable lesson right then: "Counteroffer the NO." After the tour of the "special school," Mum went back to the school she had picked for me from the get-go and asked them to reconsider. She

TURNING POINTS

wanted them to give it a try just for one week to see how it would go. If it didn't work out, she explained to them, then we would revisit the decision regarding the best school option for me.

Mum skillfully managed to turn the firm "no" into something the school officials would consider. My mum explained that I had attended Variety Village, an all-ability facility during an "Amp Camp." They worked really hard with me and all the other kids who were arm amps (amputees), to ensure we were able to tie our shoelaces, do our zippers, and all those things I would need to achieve the big success of the first day at school.

On my first day, Mum knew that in order for me to be able to stay in my neighborhood school, I had to get outside for recess like everyone else. Before I left home, Mum held my shoulders so tightly that I still remember that feeling of her firm fingers digging in. She looked me straight in the eyes and said, "Tracy, it is really important that everyone is included at recess. Do you understand? It is really important that you and all your friends are outside together at recess."

The principal told me years later that he went out looking for me at recess. I never showed up. He was devastated. After school, he intentionally waited to greet and approach my mum to help soften the blow with the bad news. They came to find me together—Mum and the principal. Mum asked me, "Tracy, did you get outside?" I looked down sadly as I had not gotten outside. The principal spoke the words for me that I could not say. I was silent because I had broken my promise and disappointed my mum. I was so sad that I couldn't speak. The principal filled the silence for me by saying, "Tracy did not get outside for recess." My mum looked at me and asked, "Is that true, Tracy?" I told her it was. They decided to speak

WHO NEEDS A HAND?

to my teacher, who regretfully confirmed that I had not been outside for recess.

My mum asked the teacher what happened, and my teacher replied, "Well, Tracy tied her shoelaces in record time. A friend beside her couldn't tie her shoelaces so Tracy helped her. Well, then it turns out that nobody could tie their shoelaces so the kids all lined up. Tracy ended up tying the shoelaces of the entire class. Tracy was bound and determined to make sure everyone was included." The teacher continued, "I don't know exactly why, but it sure was important to Tracy that nobody was left behind. By the time Tracy had finished tying the shoelaces of the entire class, recess was over."

I was sad I had broken my promise about getting outside, but also didn't want to break my other promised not to leave anyone behind. But I couldn't get the class ready before recess was over despite my best efforts.

The rest of the story is that I was given another chance to get outside for recess the next day, and I stayed in that school with my friends. I had broken my promise, but I had shown them I understood what they wanted of me and demonstrated that I had the ability. It was a sort of negotiation, and my shoe-tying skills and dedication to include everyone showed them I had what it took. This was a critical lesson in how to get where you want to go despite the apparent obstacles, and I didn't forget it, even though I was only in kindergarten. It molded my approach to getting past the many obstacles my physical limitations presented to me for the rest of my life.

I always counteroffer "no" and consistently work hard to ensure I deliver on my promises. Being more prepared than everybody else as a self-starter was a wonderful early entrepreneurial lesson to getting

TURNING POINTS

ahead. What value could I create for others to shift perception and be genuinely included?

There's another question to ponder: "How come all the other kids with hands did not have to be able to tie their shoelaces?" When policies or rules or obstacles are in your way, ask yourself how relevant they truly are to your success in your personal or professional life. How relevant was it that I could or could not tie my shoelaces? In your professional life or as an entrepreneur, ask yourself whether your standards are even relevant stopping points to advancement, for example. And as you counteroffer "no," also keep in mind that the opinion or assessment by the other party is rarely based on the full knowledge of who you are—your whole self.

Don't let such roadblocks as "no," preconceived notions by others, or stereotypes stand in your way or prevent you from moving ahead. Find a way to open that door of opportunity so they can see what you know and who you really are. Counteroffer "no" because you know you belong there! With a confident approach and a determined mindset, you will figure out how to help others see you for who you are. I went from not being allowed in a particular school based on the perception that I couldn't tie shoelaces to becoming the shoelace-tying champion.

Unstoppable Tracy Schmitt
#1 International MegaSuccess Speaker
UnstoppableTracy.com

CHAPTER NINE

Finding Yourself by Giving to Others

"Heroes represent the best of ourselves, respecting that we are human beings. A hero can be anyone from Gandhi to your classroom teacher, anyone who can show courage when faced with a problem. A hero is someone who is willing to help others in his or her best capacity."

—Enrique José Martín Morales (commonly known as Ricky Martin), Puerto Rican singer, actor, and author

"Scandi-Asian" is how I often describe myself. I started my life in Korea, born to a family who abandoned me at the age of two outside of a police station in Seoul. After spending a year in a local orphanage, I immigrated to the United States where I was adopted by a German/Norwegian couple who called the small town of Fergus Falls, Minnesota, their home. My parents weren't wealthy and were both employed as public school teachers, but they were driven, generous, and kind.

TURNING POINTS

In the months prior to my arrival, social workers and adoption counselors had primed my new American family to anticipate a period of adjustment, assuring them that transitioning an international adoptee into a new country, where everything felt unfamiliar, strange, and sometimes frightening, would present challenges. So, in the months following my arrival, my parents naturally attested my early jags of uncertainty and fear to the normal process of settling into my new surroundings. But as I grew, those momentary jags increased in frequency and duration.

At the age of 12, my periodic moments of anxiety became more frequent and eventually manifested into a deep depression. My discomfort in my own skin became unbearable, and moving through each minute felt impossible. The heaviness of trying to make it through even a single day eventually became overwhelming, and I found myself having suicidal ideations. I confided in two of my closest friends, believing that our conversations would never go beyond the three of us. But they sought help, reaching out to the school counselor and my parents, fearing I would act on my thoughts. I can still remember the looks on my parents' faces when they confronted me—they were terrified and heartsick. I assured them it was nothing, just me being dramatic and having a bad day or two. But in my mind, I told myself I would never tell anyone how I felt again, embarrassed and ashamed by what I believed was a weakness within myself.

At 15 and again at 18, I found myself emotionally sinking again, and at 21, my depression settled in so heavily that I woke up every day contemplating taking my own life. In the fall of 1992, four months after graduating with honors from college and getting engaged, I attempted suicide. From an outsider's view it made no sense. I was young, educated, and on the verge of starting a beautiful new phase

FINDING YOURSELF BY GIVING TO OTHERS

of my life. I should have been blissful and hopeful for the future. But internally I had been fighting for almost a decade to make it through every minute of every day. I was emotionally and physically depleted from keeping up the facade. My family was desperate for me to get help, so I sought counseling and began taking antidepressants, but I never fully committed to the medications in the hopes of just being "normal."

In the fall of 2009, I found myself at yet another low point, waking up in a cold sweat every night, irrationally fearing the worst, with my mind and heart racing. My father, loving but unsure of how to handle my emotional plummets, would distance himself—fearful of saying the wrong thing or unintentionally exacerbating the situation. But my mother, who over the years had become well attuned to reading the nonverbal cues of my spirals, was there for me each day—quite literally pulling me up and out of bed at times; gently but assertively making sure I ate, and driving me to and from my counselor's appointments.

When I look back at this segment of time, I feel a sense of gratitude to my mother that I will never be able to put into words. But I also remember feeling as if every day I was facing a three-kilometer, open-water swim. In my mind's eye, I could almost see everyone around me taking on the challenge with gusto—paddling and kicking through each moment of the day as if it were second nature, while I flailed and struggled through each minute.

What was wrong with me? Why couldn't I get it together and just be happy? Why couldn't I just be like everyone else? I felt the strength of my mother helping me, hoisting me along as she pushed her way through each hour for both us. But I also saw the toll it took on her and the rift that was growing with my father. Much like the panicked

TURNING POINTS

swimmers drowning in a real ocean, I felt my weight pulling down both of them, a little deeper every day. In my heart, I feared I would take them all the way down with me, and the pain of knowing how much I was hurting them was overwhelming.

At some point I began to wonder if this was how my life would be forever—if this was the roller coaster I would ride until I just couldn't take it anymore. But somewhere inside, a small part of me held onto a spark of hope that things could be different. So in the fall of 2014, I pushed myself to do something out of my comfort zone: during a season when I had become accustomed to experiencing an emotional descent, I chose to volunteer for our city's annual Out of the Darkness Suicide Prevention Walk. It seemed counterintuitive, but I think I believed that even if the trajectory of my life seemed impossible to change, perhaps I could help others who still had a chance to redirect theirs. In the months leading up to the walk event, I anticipated channeling my focus on the tasks at hand, thinking solely of the work that needed to be done. But what transpired in those months, working side by side with my peers, was transformative and unexpected: people talked about depression, talked about mental health and suicide. And they talked about it openly, without a trace of shame or judgment.

It was overwhelming, and it was freeing. I started asking myself, "What if I stopped trying to pretend that I didn't suffer from depression—what would that do to, or for, my life?" It was a question I had never really allowed myself to ponder. I began taking a different approach to my mental health and looked at it as something I needed to cognitively understand and research. I had lived with anxiety and depression for so long but never truly educated myself on it.

FINDING YOURSELF BY GIVING TO OTHERS

As I immersed myself into learning about my mental health, I found I was more open to the possibility of talking about it and acknowledging the impact it had on my life. But even more so, I finally began shedding some of the shame I had carried for having a mental illness and allowed myself to take all of the energies I had been using to hide it and re-channel them into keeping myself well. As the date of the suicide prevention walk drew closer, I found myself talking about mental health more often and more openly to people around me—including those with whom I had struggled to discuss the topic in the past, like my father. Our conversations were superficial to some extent, concentrating on the semantics of the walk, but it was progress for us, and that was promising.

For the first time, I felt something that I hadn't felt for most of my life—the possibility of gaining some small control over the emotional roller coaster that had dominated all of our lives. Then six days before the walk, my mother left me two voicemails. The first: "You need to come to the hospital, Sarah, your dad collapsed and is in a coma," and the second: "Honey I'm so sorry to tell you this over the phone. Your dad is gone." In the decades that anxiety and depression had dictated my life, death had always been in the shadows of my mind, coaxing me toward it with a promise of relief from my pain. But here, staring me in the face, it took on a vastly different form.

Over the next several days, the response from our community was immense—former students, coworkers, and friends coming forward with stories of remembrance and support. I saw and felt, for the first time, the immeasurable effect that the loss of one person can have on so many, and something inside me shifted. Six days after my father's death, my mother and I volunteered at the Out of the Darkness Walk. It was a struggle, emotionally and logistically—my

TURNING POINTS

father's wake was scheduled for later that day. But my mother and I spoke at length about our decision to participate, and she felt that he would have wanted it that way—that even though it was hard for him to say it, he was proud that I had kept fighting to live all of these years—proud that I had still kept hope—and proud that I was his daughter.

Since then my mother and I have volunteered every year for the Out of the Darkness Walks and I continue to grow in my understanding of my own mental health. It's odd sometimes to think that I feel closer to my father now than ever, but the annual walks have become a point of remembrance of my father—a place of hope for a stronger future for myself and others who battle anxiety and depression, and a reminder that even out of tremendous loss, we can find parts of ourselves that we never expected and that understanding can carry us to new places.

Sarah Dixon-Hackey
Fargo-Moorhead Out of the Darkness Chair/Army wife/Solar powered

CHAPTER TEN

Asking for Help

"Nobody stays recovered unless the life they have created is more rewarding and satisfying than the one they left behind."

—Anne Fletcher, American health and medical writer, registered dietitian

The major turning point in my life was asking for help with my addiction to alcohol. I had been drinking hard for 15 years and was getting scared about where I was headed. I had recently moved to a new city and started a new academic job. My drinking was out of control. I was so ashamed.

I asked a colleague in the school of social welfare for a referral. I had met her at an orientation for new faculty. I didn't know or trust her, but I was desperate. I asked her after having a couple of drinks. I said I wanted to see someone who was a woman and a feminist, who knew something about the academic world, but who had no ties to the university and knew something about alcohol abuse. She gave

TURNING POINTS

me a name. I called and made an appointment. That decision marks the beginning of my pivot.

My first therapy appointment was in mid-September of 1986. I approached the encounter with great fear. I was desperately in need of help, but I felt so sick with shame and guilt that I was incapable of talking honestly about myself. So I had prepared a little spiel for the therapist. I got there early. (I am compulsively early.) K, the therapist, answered the door and invited me in.

She had a modest office. I found that reassuring—her clients weren't supporting extravagance. We went in and sat down, and I started talking about myself. I told her about my recent move and new job. I told her the move had been extremely stressful for me and that I was concerned because I was drinking a little too much as a way of coping. I told her I knew the drinking wasn't helping me but I didn't seem capable of controlling it right then. I was terrified that she would condemn me then and there. But she didn't even bat an eyelash. I couldn't believe it.

For years, I had been terrified of a very critical reaction. Instead, she very calmly asked me how much I was drinking. I was honest about the amount. I could afford to be honest because my tolerance for alcohol had been changing and it no longer took as much for me to get drunk. I think I said that I drank a little more than a pint of vodka a day. I was unable to be honest about how long this had been a problem for me or about the severity of the problem. I said I had never had a blackout, but I didn't realize then how much this gave away. If I hadn't had a blackout, I certainly wouldn't have brought it up.

The truth was that I drank until I blacked out almost every night. And then K asked me about alcohol use in my family. Within that first appointment she identified me as an adult child of an alcoholic. She gave me a book to read, which was the first literature I ever read

ASKING FOR HELP

on alcoholism. In the past, when I thought about reading something, I was always too ashamed. I thought the librarian or the book store clerk would look at me and know.

Interspersed in our first conversation were lots of questions. I wanted to know which school of psychotherapy she practiced and if she ever dismissed patients because they were cured. I wanted her to know I hadn't sought help before because I doubted I could find a therapist who was smarter than me. I wanted her to know I had done a lot of thinking about the foundations of psychology and that I knew psychotherapy was more of an art than a science. I wanted her to know I wasn't going to be a pushover—that I wasn't going to be easy. I was scared.

As I left that first session with my book on alcoholism, K assured me that she could help me. She told me my problems were of the sort that responded very well to treatment. I believed her. That was just enough for me to hold onto.

For the next six weeks, I continued to drink. I saw K once a week and she gently began the process of educating me about alcoholism. I could only read the book she had loaned me after having a couple of drinks. I gradually started to realize that this was my last hurrah—my best chance to change what was happening.

At first, I thought maybe she could change me so that I could control my drinking. But K was very firm that I had to stop drinking. She didn't deliver any ultimatums, nor did she ever call me an alcoholic. But whenever I brought up the subject, she was explicit that the drinking needed to stop. The reading and our discussions really opened my eyes to the alcoholism in my family.

At that point I was willing to entertain the idea that my father was an alcoholic. His drinking problem became apparent to me when

TURNING POINTS

he was diagnosed as a diabetic and couldn't stop his drinking. But that had only happened in the last few years. I thought that for most of his life he had just been a heavy drinker. In fact, much of time I thought I was crazy to think he had a problem at all.

Through the literature on alcoholism, I learned that most of what had really bothered me about my father was due to his alcoholism. I learned that his alcoholism made him emotionally unavailable, rigid, inflexible, controlling, moody, and angry. I couldn't believe the alcoholism was so pervasive. I thought it only affected him when he was drunk. As I learned more I also started to see that I was just like him. The very things that bothered me about him were the same things that I hated in myself. I am so grateful for that insight. I am glad my own alcoholism had become so painful for me that I could no longer deny its existence.

And then my mother came to visit. The subject of alcohol was taboo in my family, and it was never to be discussed. I felt completely suspended between alternate realities during the time my mother was in town. When I next saw K I told her I needed more help. I was getting desperate. She suggested that I start attending some 12-step meetings for adult children of alcoholics. I told her the 12-step programs would not work for me, but that if I were to go to one it should be one for alcoholics. She calmly produced a copy of the local meeting schedule and circled two women's meetings—one on Wednesday and one on Friday. She told me to treat it as a research project. I couldn't say no to that.

That night I went home and got drunk. There was nothing memorable about the evening. By that time, alcohol had ceased to give me much pleasure. I just remember getting quietly, pathetically drunk. That was the last time I drank. I got up the next morning and poured out the rest of my bottle of vodka. I really wanted to stop drinking,

ASKING FOR HELP

but I didn't think there was a chance in hell that I could stop. I was still willing to give it a try. That was a Wednesday.

When it came time to go to the meeting, I went to a movie. I discovered that I had a tremendous resistance to going to self-help meetings for alcoholics. By Friday afternoon, I knew that I had to get myself to that meeting. I couldn't go back to see K having missed both opportunities. I called an acquaintance and asked him if he would walk over to the meeting with me.

Going to that first meeting was one of the most difficult things I have ever done. I felt so ashamed of myself, so degraded and debased. I couldn't believe I had sunk so low.

It was the night of Halloween. On the way to the meeting, I saw a little kid with a mask. I desperately wanted that mask—needed to hide. I was exposed, vulnerable, and raw without the shield of alcohol to protect me.

We got to the meeting place and the door was locked. I couldn't believe my luck. I stood there and thanked a God I didn't believe in for this small miracle. But then I noticed a doorbell. With a sinking heart, I rang the bell. A woman answered the door and with feet of lead, I went through that door. This marked the beginning of my recovery.

I left the meeting knowing deep within me that I was indeed an alcoholic. I had absolutely no more doubt about it. I have since known many people who struggled greatly in coming to that realization about themselves. I am grateful that I was in such pain that I could no longer struggle with denial about this basic fact. But I still felt intense shame and guilt. I didn't know what I was going to do, but I did know that I was going to try as hard as possible not to pick up a drink.

When I saw K the next week, I told her that I hadn't had a drink for a week. I said that I had headaches in the afternoons. I knew that I was detoxing; I thought maybe it was the sugar. I also told her I had gone to a meeting. But I didn't really want to talk about it.

When Wednesday night rolled around, I went to the other women's meeting. I was afraid to do much except stare at the floor and long to be invisible, but at the beginning of the meeting, someone asked if there were any newcomers. I said my name and that I was an alcoholic. That was the first time I'd ever said that out loud. I practically choked on the word. It felt awful—like a personal failure. It was tremendously difficult for me to have gone to either of those 12-step meetings; and at the time, I thought my pain and humiliation outweighed any possible benefit.

When I next saw K, I told her that I had done my research but I didn't really think self-help groups were for me. K gently but firmly said that I needed to check it out more thoroughly. She asked me why I would want to do this all by myself when I could have friends helping me. Friends? I didn't think I shared much in common with folks at those meetings, and I didn't think anyone could help me, or even like me. But I understood that my going to meetings was a condition of my continuing in therapy. And this was the first time I contemplated the idea that getting sober was a collective action.

I continued in therapy for six years, and I received lots of help and support from the people in 12-step programs. I have now been enjoying a sober life for 31 years.

Looking back, getting sober has been the most significant accomplishment of my life. And it all started with reaching outside of my shame and asking for help.

C.M., Ph.D
Sober feminist warrior/Mother/Athlete

CHAPTER ELEVEN

From Survivor to Victor

"We cannot change anything until we accept it. Condemnation does not liberate, it oppresses."

—Carl Gustav Jung, Swiss psychiatrist and psychoanalyst
(July 26, 1875–June 6, 1961)

Before I left him, it was like I was infected with an uneasiness that resided in the pit of my stomach and radiated all the way to the root endings of my every nerve. Sometimes the feeling was subtle and other times it could almost catapult me into a severe panic attack. No matter how hard I tried to shove it into the back of my mind during interims of peace, those feelings always stayed with me. I would find myself obsessing over the thought of when another eruption might occur. I wondered what unsuspecting action would send him into a tailspin, a fit of jealous rage, or an arsenal of accusations. How much more of my aching spirit could be devoured? I didn't feel like myself anymore. And the worst part wasn't being the victim of domestic violence; it was that my sense of identity was slipping away.

TURNING POINTS

I remember making that final split-second decision as I dialed my sister's number. We had been planning a rummage sale for quite some time, but I had a newly developed strategy to sell off most of my things and use that money to start my life over with my one-year-old daughter. Having taken a muddy, rutted path through life herself, there was no question that my sister was going to help me escape the nightmare that had become my everyday life. She was much older than I was and had disappeared from our lives for over seven years when I was very young. During that time everyone thought she was dead, but I never believed that. Having her back in my life was a true blessing and I knew she would help me escape my personal hell.

What they say is true. Most women repeatedly return to their abusers as if they're gluttons for punishment, and I was no exception. I had already divorced the guy but had returned with higher hopes for the next time around. I never thought, in a million years, that I was the type of woman who would end up in a violent relationship, but again, no woman wants to believe that.

I remember my father being shocked when I finally told him what had been happening. He said he didn't think domestic abuse was possible with instincts like mine. But it hadn't been a malfunction of my instincts; it was the fact that I had ignored them. The first red flag should've been the whirlwind romance and the sudden engagement that was supposed to be drawn out, but I had been enticed by a tropical wedding within months of meeting him. I had also become pregnant, so a sudden marriage seemed like the right thing to do. I had met his family almost immediately and they seemed charming and kind. He was handsome and successful and appeared to be doing very nice things for people; even the business that he owned assisted the disabled. He appeared to be a saint, but I found out the hard way that not all that glitters is gold. Something always felt off, but I couldn't put my finger on it prior to the first incident.

The first time I was assaulted wasn't long after all the wedding plans had been made, deposits paid, and airline tickets purchased. We had been at a concert where the lead singer was a friend of a friend and I said hello to him after the show without introducing my fiancé, which caused all hell to break loose. Before I knew it, we were in his SUV after our dispute where I had defended my actions and he waited until we were alone to grab the back of my neck and hair and slam the top of my head into the dashboard. I remember being stunned and crawling into the back seat. As he drove he told me he was going to kill me and throw me in the river. I had never feared for my life before, but from that day forward I would fear for my life on a daily basis.

This story isn't about my dark days. It's a story about how I survived and finally found peace and prosperity in my life. But to arrive at that plateau, I first had to go through more heartache. My unborn child was diagnosed with a birth defect called gastroschisis, where the stomach wall remains open and exposes the intestines, which become inflamed from the amniotic fluid that my body was barely producing. I was ordered on bedrest very early in my pregnancy, so between my health condition and the fact that my only income was derived from his business—or let me rephrase that: not income but small allowances that he would dictate how I could spend. I was now 100-percent dependent upon him.

On the day my daughter was born, her father left the hospital to go out partying and sometime after he had returned, I had a night terror where I saw my infant, with no life supports, dying, but I couldn't help her. I was locked in a sleep paralysis and only half conscious until I finally figured out how to speak and I cried for him to turn

TURNING POINTS

the light on. Before I could explain, he immediately called me a psycho and started yelling at me. I reached for the phone to call a nurse and he grabbed it out of my hands and hit me right in the stomach with it where I just had had an emergency C-section. I had him removed from the hospital shortly thereafter.

My life was going down the drain, but the only thing I cared about was the health of my child. One of the nurses in the NICU, where my daughter spent the first six weeks of her life on a respirator and feeding tubes while morphine was pumped into her tiny veins, told me my daughter's was the worst case of gastroschisis she had ever seen. I single-handedly made all of the life-and-death decisions for my child. Her first surgery failed, and her organs had begun to shut down. It had been several weeks since her birth, and I still had not been permitted to hold her in my arms. It was unclear if I would ever get that chance. I remained steadfast for her. At that point, I recognized that we both were fighters. Her second surgery was successful, and I was eventually able to take her home one month after this ordeal began.

Back to the rummage sale, with my by then one-year-old daughter: after the sale was over, I packed just what I needed for myself and my daughter, and we escaped. We were headed straight into the unknown, but it was better than living in a guaranteed hell. I only had $400 to my name and not even a vehicle of my own since I had gotten into a car accident only months before. My sister and her family opened their home to my daughter and me and even though there was so much uncertainty, living with her brought me so much joy. I knew I was called by a higher power to go live with her and learn about what had happened to her during those seven lost years. It was probably one of the most significant decisions I had ever made, especially since she was killed in a car accident just months after I moved out of her home. My time with her was precious and I got to know her as I never had before.

FROM SURVIVOR TO VICTOR

Even after escaping my ex-husband, life wouldn't stop delivering heavy doses of loss and anguish. Within two years, I had shattered my knee in a car accident. I had lost my grandmother, my uncle, and my sister. And my niece, my sister's daughter, had nearly been killed in a separate car accident.

It's not what life brings forth; it's how a person absorbs what is delivered and the attitude they maintain. Sometimes I think it was harder for the people close to me, who were looking in at my life, than it was for me—I was simply looking ahead. Even with all of the despair, I was becoming a more evolved version of myself. I was studying under a very effective natural healer, I had finished my bachelor of arts degree, I was working toward my associate's degree in massage therapy, raising and selling wolfdogs, and working at a high-end restaurant. I didn't choose just one but instead had implemented all of my passions. Life was too precious to waste.

I refused to get a conventional job and instead pursued my vision of erecting a home healthcare business. I'm sure people thought I was all talk, but anyone who knows me well knows that I follow through with my visions. I have since built a thriving, healthy corporation and raised the most kind-hearted daughter a mother could ever ask for. I count my blessings every day and praise my Creator for the life lessons I struggled to learn.

And the greatest gift is that I know who I am because of all I have gone through.

Lesley Barry
Entrepreneur/CEO/Forward thinker
Good Life Services Inc.

CHAPTER TWELVE

I Am Not Going This Way Alone

"Have I not commanded you? Be strong and courageous. Do not be afraid; do not be discouraged, for the LORD your God will be with you wherever you go."

—Joshua 1:9 (Holy Bible, New International Version (NIV))

I still remember when my nightmares ended. But first I need to tell you how they began. I was a good kid, a middle child, raised in a faithful home with loving parents. My dad coached football in a small town in Minnesota, and I was active in everything at school, but my passion was sports. As a young person I loved God and would share my thoughts with Him in my diary. I didn't realize what that faith foundation was going to mean to my life until my life was turned upside down on August 11, 1979.

I was 18 and ready to play basketball at my parents' alma mater. Just weeks before the start of college, a drunk teen driver barreled through an intersection. Two people died and I suffered a broken neck and a mild traumatic brain injury. I was in and out of consciousness for the next five weeks. When I finally understood what had happened, I held fast to my faith. *God is going with me*, I told myself repeatedly. *I will meet this challenge like I did other challenges.* Even so, it hurt to miss my freshman year at Concordia College in Moorhead, Minnesota. I spent three months at a hospital in Fargo, North Dakota, where as a quadriplegic, I was dependent on others for almost everything.

My days were positive with love and support from family and hometown, but my nights were restless with nightmares. One particular day I was in occupational therapy, listening to the Concordia College Chapel service on the radio, when reality hit. Here I was in a hospital struggling to feed myself with adaptive equipment instead of playing basketball and immersing myself in the college scene. I broke down crying. I called Concordia's campus pastor, who met with me that night. He told me there would be many more times when I would feel frustrated, hurt, and even angry at God. He encouraged me to imagine God so close that I could beat on His chest with my fists to release my anger. That's exactly what I did. And my nightmares ended. There were going to be some challenging days ahead, but I knew I was not alone.

Adapting to my new life as a quadriplegic demanded every bit of the stamina I had needed to run those countless "lady-killer" basketball drills, and the discipline and determination from sports helped me to soldier through three months of rehab at the renowned Craig Rehabilitation Hospital in Denver. My spinal cord was not severed, so parts of my muscles functioned throughout my body, but I didn't know how much strength would come back. With my dominant right hand paralyzed, I had to learn to do everything with only my left hand. I threw myself into therapy, knowing I needed as much strength as possible for a life of greater independence.

In fall 1980, I became a full-time student at Concordia. I remember one day during my freshman year when I wrestled with intense anger during my workout. Why didn't God hear my prayers? If you are out there, God, just touch me, my heart cried. Later that day, I received a call from a professor telling me a ticket was provided for me to hear Cheryl Prewitt, Miss America 1980, speak that night. I put on my best suit and went. She, too, had survived a horrific car accident and she later received a faith healing. She said God can heal us if we have faith. At the end of the program, I told her how angry I had been that very day and asked how I could know what God wanted for my life. I had no idea how God could use me in a wheelchair. She told me the only way I could know was to get into His word. She got her Bible and wrote out Jeremiah 29:11, which tells how the plans God has for me are for good, and not for evil, to give me a future and a hope. Even though there was going to be some pain and tears along the way, I now knew there was a plan. And I clung to that verse!

The last day of my freshman year, I went to the gym to do a quick workout. I put my braces on and I began to walk with my walker. Walker, step, swing leg. Repeat. My legs were striding out with greater ease than ever before and at first, I thought I had been healed! Then my back started to hurt. But I pressed on to complete 12 laps, a mile, and I crashed to the floor just two steps before I reached my power wheelchair. I believed that day that the strength to walk that mile came from a power outside of me. I felt that God was saying you're not there yet, but I am with you all the way. I will give you strength. The next day, my walking returned to my usual slow and effortful pace, but that miraculous event motivated me throughout

TURNING POINTS

my college years. I overcame my fears of stepping out and walking short distances with a cane or forearm crutches, whether it was in class or at a restaurant. I walked across the stage at graduation because I had the ability to do it and the courage to be me.

After college, I completed my master's degree in social work. Even with these accomplishments, part of me still missed the joy of sports. I focused on my career as a rehab social worker, working with families affected by disability at the same Fargo hospital where I had been a patient. Then someone asked me to try quad rugby. I knew little about sports for people with disabilities, so I was intrigued. This crazy sport with wheelchairs crashing and bodies flying thrilled me and later, in 1993, led me to try wheelchair racing.

Training, traveling, and competing throughout the country as a wheelchair athlete gave me a new level of confidence. I trained hard and three years later, I competed on an elite level at the 1996 Paralympics in Atlanta. One year later I set four national records, of which one still stands today. It was far beyond what I could have imagined! In support of my racing, my employer became an official Olympic sponsor and changed my job to athlete/ambassador. In this role, I spoke nationwide and developed local support programs for individuals and families affected by disability. I even wrote a book. I wanted to help others reach their dreams and became involved with Wheels for the World, an international disability outreach of Joni Eareckson Tada, which provides refurbished wheelchairs. My racing career ended abruptly at the 2000 Paralympics in Sydney, Australia, when I tore a tendon in my wrist.

My 20-year healthcare career ended when my job was cut during a series of layoffs, but God blessed me with a job as director of women's ministries at my church. I began volunteering with Hope

I AM NOT GOING THIS WAY ALONE

Inc., a local nonprofit that provides recreational opportunities for children with mobility challenges. I enjoyed cheering them on and seeing them gain confidence through sports. A few years later, the leader asked me to join the new adult softball team. Fear clutched me. I was in my 50s by then. I had to protect myself. I couldn't throw like I used to throw and I couldn't catch like I used to catch. I only had one good hand. I could get hurt!

Then I realized I had to practice what I preached. It wasn't about being *the* best. It was about being *your* best and using what God has given you. I knew I had to try, but I also knew I needed to be wise. I asked another leader to play catch with me to see if I could handle the ball. And I could! I could do this! I joined the team and I felt that joy return to me. I am a people person, a positive person, and a person of faith. And I am also a person who delights in sports. Because softball was a mountain-top experience, I tried sled hockey. I knew how important every single person on the team was. Even though I had to have someone push my sled and my sticks were duct-taped to my hands, I was in the game! It's not always graceful. It's not always pretty. But it's so much fun!

After my accident I learned it was okay to cry. Over the years, God healed my broken heart as I learned to turn my prayers to Him. When I'm tempted to be afraid to try new things and to stay safe in the chair, I remind myself that I'm not going this way alone. And yes, the plans He has for me are for good, and not for evil, to give me a future and a hope. My life is blessed.

Judy Siegle
Two-time Paralympian/Speaker/Author
JudySiegle.com

CHAPTER THIRTEEN

Plan B Was My Best Choice

"Success in life is not how well we execute Plan A; it's how smoothly we cope with Plan B."

—Sarah Ban Breathnach, American best-selling author, philanthropist, and public speaker

As far back as I can remember, I have always wanted to be a health professional. My mom worked in our local district hospital as a nurse. And the young me was always fascinated when she would come home with some pills or syrups for us. How could she guess we needed this one or that one, and how come it always worked? I wanted to do the same. It was magical. But when I got into 10th grade, where (according to our school system at that time) we could take the option of becoming a nurse, I was then old enough to tell myself that I should be a medical doctor instead of a nurse. School was easy for me, and I had no doubt I would be admitted to medical school if I applied. I was driven and wanted to aim higher. I was accepted to medical school and almost zoomed through it. But when

TURNING POINTS

my class was doing the required internship, our country (Burundi) experienced civil political unrest. It made the two years of internship more stressful than the first years of medical school.

By the time I got my degree as a general practitioner, I had already decided to relocate to the neighboring country (Rwanda) that was rebuilding after the 1994 genocide. Rwanda was becoming more and more stable by the time I decided to move there, although serious political upheavals were still occurring. I had relatives there, so it was a smooth transition as they helped me get acclimated. One year into practice, I decided to join the first cohort of general practitioners who would train in-country to become medical specialists. My heart was into pediatrics but remembering how painful it was for me to see babies crying when in pain and I was unable to help them while I was an intern, I decided that I would be happier helping mothers giving birth. Not only could I contribute to that happiness of welcoming a beautiful addition within a family, but also, I would get to hold babies. Another part of me was convinced that as a woman I would relate more and better, helping women in need of a gynecologist or an obstetrician.

Friends, some of them already in the profession, tried to discourage me. Some told me this was not a job for a woman. They also said that being an ob-gyn was too demanding and physically taxing. I would not listen. I was single at that time and could not grasp how being a wife/mother might interfere with what my heart wanted so dearly. I took and passed my test and got accepted into residency. Two years into residency, I got married and later on, had my first baby. My husband was not living in the same city. His job took him 70 kilometers away, and he could only come home on weekends every two or three weeks. My training included one year abroad, and I went with my six-month-old baby girl. I managed to finish that year without mental breakdown, surprisingly.

The last year of training was the hardest. Here I was with an 18-month-old baby, still in residency with all it requires in terms of night duties, without any kind of family support. I had left my family in Burundi, the country I was living in was just recovering from a devastating war, and my relatives were just trying to bring things back to normal for their families. We would hear a lot of stories of grown men sexually abusing young girls, even babies. And I would sometimes receive those toddlers while in the outpatient department. It was draining and quite frightening, thinking that I had a kid that age who could also be a victim, if I was to just leave her with a nanny at home. (It's not unusual to have both a nanny and a male helper for middle and upper class in many developing countries.)

My situation wasn't working. It was draining. The pressure was just too much. To add to this, I had developed a serious back problem from the time when I was pregnant and had to spend nights on my feet delivering babies. We would frequently do three to five caesarean sections per night.

That is when I started thinking about leaving clinical practice and joining public health. It was a very tough decision. I got zero support. No one understood what I was going through. For my husband, I had to continue with the clinical practice for a while longer, in hopes that things would settle eventually. He could not change his job location. It was not easy for him. For my family in town, it was a disappointment. I have always been that smart kid of whom they were all proud. And in a setting where there were not enough

TURNING POINTS

doctors, I was that link everyone needed to get proper care, regardless of the medical field.

The same reaction came from my friends. For the government, it was simply unacceptable: The need for specialists in clinical practice was acute. They could not afford to lose me. Many of these arguments were valid and they added to my feelings of guilt. The most difficult for me was that I felt like a loser! In my head, only smart people do medical school and treat people. I had to fight with my pride and my ego. While in medical school, we use to joke that the less smart medical students would become public health specialists. In addition to everything happening in my head and around me regarding that decision, I couldn't stop thinking and worrying about all the people I would disappoint.

I felt trapped into something I no longer could do but couldn't escape. As I continued to struggle with the impossible situation, I found myself talking to my little girl, telling her what was going on. She was three years old. There was no way she could comprehend. But I felt she was the only one I had left who would listen. During our conversations over dinner, I came to understand that it was about my health and my baby's well-being. No one from the outside could make that decision for me. Everyone felt entitled to criticize my career move, but no one was ready to extend a helping hand to ease my situation or offer alternative solutions. And becoming a prisoner of my own pride was not smart at all.

When I realized how much of my dilemma was my own pride, suddenly the decision I needed to make was clear. I left clinical practice and joined public health. It took six years and the birth of a second child before my husband was able to reunite with us and work from the same town we all lived in. I can't imagine having stayed all those

PLAN B WAS MY BEST CHOICE

years with clinical practice under all those circumstances, family and personal. In hindsight, I know that was the best decision I could have made, and I couldn't make it until I realized what the true priorities were. I have never been happier or more balanced, professionally and personally.

Dr. A.M.
International consultant/Maternal and
newborn health advocate/Avid reader

CHAPTER FOURTEEN

Feeling Powerful and Empowered

"The only way to deal with an unfree world is to become so absolutely free that your very existence is an act of rebellion."

—Albert Camus, French philosopher, author, and journalist

If someone were to describe me up until the beginning of 2013, they would more likely say that I was a hard-nosed conservative with strict, traditional beliefs. I didn't really value nor respect uniqueness or individuality. Today, I hope people would say I am a passionate woman who is impacting the community positively. They might also state that I have a wardrobe of pretty dresses and that I have progressed to value people over politics. The road to getting where I currently am, as a person, was long and unconventional. I had to go through many losses before making the decision to transition from being a man to becoming a woman, which also meant no longer being a stakeholder to male privilege.

TURNING POINTS

In early 2013, I was married to a woman who shared my religious beliefs and political leanings. My turning point started after losing both my grandparents. My grandmother passed away first and, just one month later, my grandfather died. I had driven my grandparents to many chemotherapy appointments and I knew this was probably coming. Still, the loss hurt very badly. A month after we laid my grandparents to rest, my mother was diagnosed with cancer, the same type that killed her mother. While I was still mourning and praying for answers to make sense of all that was happening, I lost a great friend who was younger than me due to a brain tumor. His death impacted me much differently than other deaths prior to that time. I felt indescribable sorrow.

Something else happened as I was processing this particular death. I realized that the cultural norms of my childhood never allowed me to really have deep or real feelings. That was the beginning of many more recognitions that would rattle me to my core and change my perspective on nearly everything.

I started to accept truths that had not registered as clearly in my young and "invincible" mind, such as the fact that everything expires and that one day I was going to die, too. There was a chance I might not be ready for that moment when it happens. I also realized that if I were to die now, I would regret how I had lived my life.

Thus, I made an admission to myself that I had not been telling myself the truth and I needed to start pursuing a real, authentic life. Something was totally misaligned.

I found myself revisiting the feelings that just the thought of wearing a dress brought to my heart. Yes, this simple, trivial detail for many (wearing a dress) meant the world to me. From a young age, I loved wearing dresses, but my early memories were always associated

FEELING POWERFUL AND EMPOWERED

with my parents getting mad. The very first time it happened, they blamed my older brother because they thought I was too young to put it on by myself. During my puberty years and until I was probably thirteen, I secretly cross-dressed at least once a month, including taking home a prom dress from the "lost-and-found" pile at school. I would make a resolution to quit cross-dressing and I would even stop, but I never made it more than six months. I would greatly miss the wonderful feeling this "forbidden" gesture brought to my entire existence.

I needed to reconcile my inner truth and how I lived my life: as a woman caged in a male body. However, I was extremely depressed at that time and unable to unclutter my mind. I often felt paralyzed and with no guidance on how to free myself. At my lowest emotional point, the many feelings I had repressed for so long came rushing into my being at the core. The sexual abuse I suffered as a child resurfaced. This old demon reemerged while I was trying to go through the mourning process of the friend who had passed away and as I was making resolutions to be true in the way I lived my life.

I would often feel so strange in my own body. Almost like I was a guest in the visible male shell I wore. During childhood and puberty, I couldn't imagine growing up to become a man and the mere thought of myself as a man felt so wrong. I was terrified by that idea. I couldn't even envision how I would look. I remember frequently staring at myself in a mirror for long periods of time, from eight years old up until I was 21, and being stunned by my own developing masculinity. It was almost like I would be looking at someone else's reflection. I felt like a freak.

Unfortunately, I did not feel supported by my faith community and consistently experienced the rarely spoken about and often

TURNING POINTS

unrecognized negative aspects of narrowed religious views. Naming the denomination I was affiliated with is irrelevant as I realize this could happen in any faith community.

I was in such despair that I felt killing myself would save my family the embarrassment of having such an odd person as me associated with them. However faithless I had become, though, I didn't want to die. In this spiritual crisis that I was also undergoing, I thought death meant eternal blackness and that scared me. In a panicked moment, I got up without much thought and ran to my computer to order myself a purple dress on Amazon. I didn't stop there. I also ordered heels and other female shoes in my size. As crazy as that sounds, this reaction saved me from taking my own life. I had tried on clothing from my soon-to-be ex-wife's closet, but her clothes were a little too small.

The outfit came two days after I placed the order. I couldn't wait to try everything on and look in the mirror to see my own reflection. I was glowing! Nearly a decade later, I could see much clearer. There was nothing wrong with me. As I began a long healing process, I started to see for the first time what I wanted to do in my life and what my future could look like. The path seemed very wide open and well-lit for me. I needed to share this with someone. It made sense that I would start with telling my wife at the time about what was going on with my new-found gender realization.

As difficult as it was, I told my wife or rather, soon-to-be ex-wife, about my cross-dressing and explained to her the confusion I grew up with around cross-dressing—namely that I was molested repeatedly by a young man who felt he had the right to abuse me because I wore women's clothing. I told her the association of the sexual abuse with the clothing I enjoyed had always been perplexing to

FEELING POWERFUL AND EMPOWERED

me and that I had finally sorted through those messy feelings. I had concluded that there was no connection between those two pieces.

Eventually, I also told her that I had recently bought some female garments as I was feeling lost, but when I tried them on, it felt like I had found myself. I told her . . . and this was difficult . . . that I was cross-dressing in private because I needed more time to understand what that really meant and to process everything. I was as honest and truthful with her as I could be about what I felt.

She was stunned. As I waited for her to say something—anything—she got up and went in the bathroom, shut the door, and locked herself in without a single word. After two hours of listening to her talking on the phone and not being able to hear exactly what she was saying or who she was talking with, she came out of the bathroom. The next thing I witnessed was my soon-to-be ex-wife emerging from the bedroom with a bag and walking out of our apartment door, without even acknowledging that I was still there.

Two weeks later, she came back for the first time since her departure. She was back to tell me she was leaving for good and that I needed professional help. Her mother came with her. Her mother proceeded to scold me as she handed me the divorce papers on behalf of her daughter. One thing that will be hard to forget is the noise of disdain and disgust she made as she looked at me. I can't even describe that noise, but it was an unmistakable sound that made me feel simply despicable. As they left the apartment, they told me that I had 48 hours to gather my belongings and vacate.

This was another low point of my life, when I felt I everyone would be better off if I died. In my head, I was convinced there was no purpose for my existence, that my birth was just a result of happenstance.

TURNING POINTS

In the days following my wife's walkout, I again contemplated the idea that my parents would be better off with a dead son than an alive, transgender daughter. I also concluded (in my head) that in the grander scheme of things, I didn't really matter. Not knowing how to proceed through life with all that darkness inside and around me, I decided to log on to the transgender social site where I had posted my first and only picture several weeks before to find out where to buy female fashion items. My goal was to delete the account because I didn't want my parents, after my passing, ever to find out I was a transgender person. I didn't want to ruin every memory they had of me. As I opened the account, I realized I had five new messages. This made my stress, my anxiety, and my depression go away for five seconds. I convinced myself to read the messages. After all, it would not take that much time and I could spare five minutes.

"Hey lady, welcome, I see you're hiding your face a little, but you look super cute," was the opening message. It was the first time someone had called me a lady and it was relieving. The statement offered a contrast to what else was happening. It felt like drinking a glass of cold water on a hot day. The noise of a million judgments I had held onto since my childhood fell silent for once. As I sat there reflecting, I felt every distorted thought and rationalization around gender identity from others lose their power. That judging little voice and the condemning rhetoric I grew up to believe were being replaced by an affirming voice. This was the first time I "heard" this voice as clear as it sounded: "Am I the lady everyone is talking about?" From my deepest soul it resounded a very endorsing "YES, I AM." The weight of so many people's opinions fell off my shoulders. I was finally ready to start truly healing and chasing my dreams. I was alive, I chose to be, and I was going to start living my life to its fullest.

FEELING POWERFUL AND EMPOWERED

In 2015, I made the bold decision to move forward publicly in the world as the real me: a woman. It was amazing how light the hem of my purple dress felt as I stepped into the annual Pride Center meeting. It was a potluck and the people were as unique as the dishes they brought. There was so much beauty and support around me. After that, I started making frequent appearances as myself—a woman—in dresses that made me feel empowered.

It seems so petty to feel empowered by dresses, but wearing my chosen clothing makes me feel so light. Sometimes, I feel like I could fly.

Buying a white wedding dress to be married later in 2015 was an exciting time. I was ecstatic to become someone's partner and be fully embraced with all my uniqueness. The whole shopping process, trying the dress on, etc., was very affirming. I finally felt like I belonged somewhere in the world and I was beautiful. My wedding experience solidified for me the fact that my life had made a 180-degree turn and my path would never be the same. And I couldn't be more grateful!

Rebel Marie
M.S. in Agency and Mental Health Counseling
Human rights activist/Gardner

CHAPTER FIFTEEN

Losing My Job and Finding Myself

"There will always be rocks in the road ahead of us.
They will be stumbling blocks or stepping stones;
it all depends on how you use them."

—Friedrich Wilhelm Nietzsche, German philosopher, cultural critic,
composer, poet, philologist, Latin and Greek scholar
(October 15, 1844–August 25, 1900)

As I sat in the human resources director's office, listening to her and my supervisor tell me, "Your team has lost faith in you," I felt an ocean of indescribable emotions at the deepest of my core. It seemed like my professional world and my ego were instantly and simultaneously crushed into a million pieces that could not possibly be salvaged. This organization had been part of my life in some capacity or another since my arrival into the United Stated of America as a refugee, almost 18 years prior.

TURNING POINTS

Sick to my stomach, I listened to both authority figures in my professional life go through a litany of the reasons why I had to either resign on the spot or be terminated. My body reacted in a way that I could not control. A torrent of tears started flowing on my cheeks, even though I was trying very hard to "be strong" and go through that meeting as gracefully as possible and with minimal emotions that would seem "unprofessional." Controlling my body could not be accomplished intellectually. There was a total disconnect between my heart and my brain at that moment and the only reaction my heart directed me to do was to cry. Profusely.

I had never been fired before. At 47 years old, I had held eight to ten professional jobs, either on a part-time or full-time basis. Sitting in front of my supervisor and the human resources director for this reason was a completely new terrain, absolutely uncharted ground for me. I wanted the session to be over. Internally, I was invoking *Imana* and all the saints in heaven to inspire them to just move to the next step instead of beating around the bush, since they had already mentioned the only two options: resigning now or being terminated.

When one of them finally asked me what I wanted to do, I felt momentary relief from their excruciating, incriminating monologue. It gave me some type of control over what was happening. Truth be told, all this was an illusion. Yes, it was a perceived sense of control over how I wanted to be kicked in the behind or how I wanted to be thrown under the bus.

If I was expected to make a decision on the spot, could I have used a "life line," aka calling my husband (who happens to be an attorney) for some advice? Yes. Could I have had a few minutes to research electronically all the pros and cons of being fired versus being terminated? Absolutely—I had never considered making this kind of decision. How do you even make such a life-altering decision in a split second and under duress? Were these two "choices" really the only options? Why couldn't there be another way to resolve the situation at hand?

The internal dialog I was having with myself reminded me that if I "accepted" to be fired or "terminated" (to use my interlocutors' more politically correct term), I would jeopardize the chances to be eligible for unemployment benefits. Besides, my future job search could suffer from that kind of reputation. But I also remembered that I did not take that particular job with this specific agency for the admittedly low pay it offered. Besides, it became clear to me that I lived in a small community and I trusted the professional relationships I had developed over the years. I had no doubt that those who truly knew me would still hire me for a job if I met the criteria, regardless of how I parted ways with my previous employer. You do not need to be an expert to understand that office politics can be a major reason in hiring and firing employees. The ability to collect unemployment benefits and the prospect of another job in the future were easily and quickly dismissed as deciding factors on whether I would resign by force or be terminated.

Flashing back to 15 years ago, as a single parent, a decision like this would have been undoubtedly based on the possibility to retain some kind of revenue to cover the bills. I was briefly and quickly overcome with gratitude for being in such a position of privilege where a life-changing decision would not affect my lifestyle whatsoever. My daughter would still get private violin lessons, stay on the lacrosse team, and join her French class friends on an already planned school trip to Europe. We would still be able to afford a new outfit here and there for her speech competitions without sacrifice. All these "luxurious" expenses would have been out of reach

TURNING POINTS

for my son's extracurricular activities, who was at my daughter's age 15 years ago. Funnily enough, my son would have never chosen so many involvements anyway. A happy accident, as I realized later. When my son was in high school, I wouldn't have had the finances nor the time to support him the way I could with my daughter.

Here I was, thinking about the fact that I couldn't afford even the essentials a few years ago, even while working more than two jobs at a time. Today, the annual family ski vacation plans could still happen, regardless of my employment status. Paycheck or no paycheck for me, my family lifestyle would not be impacted. Somehow, while this was a relief, it didn't change my emotional reaction. It hurt so badly I was still crying, which added to the humiliation I felt.

The disappointment, the shock, and the hurt were overwhelming. I would be lying if I said that I knew, at that moment, what decision would "harm" me less—that is, affect my ego the least.

"I will resign," I heard myself utter. I just wanted this ordeal to be over. I found myself buying into the blame these two people laid on me, not only during this meeting but also in the weeks prior. It was no surprise to me at this point that I found myself apologizing for things I strongly believe were not entirely my fault, now that I have had time to carefully process the situation from a geographic and emotional distance.

I was handed a piece of paper to make my verbal proclamation official by putting it in writing, signing, and dating it. The human resources director then told me what information would be later sent to me by mail and asked me to hand over the program credit card in my possession as well as the building keys. Both items were supposed to be turned in right away. I took the electronic employee identification key card off the collar of my blouse and handed it to my now ex-employer. I felt that I was handing her my dignity.

The director and my former supervisor briefly debated when I could collect my belongings, since they now had to accompany me in the building. My supervisor allowed me to take a two-hour break outside the building, at my request, before I could return to pack everything that was not the agency's property.

At the end of the meeting that would change my life in an unexpected way, I went back to the office that used to be mine, grabbed the program credit card from my purse, and took it back to my former supervisor before heading out for my break. As I drove on the gravel road of a nearby town without any destination in mind, I listened to relaxing music, still in shock, and allowed tears to roll freely down my face without any inhibition. As overwhelmed as I was, I couldn't decide whether I was sad or relieved. In a very weird way, I felt free.

It was a powerful, cathartic moment that reminded me of a previous life experience that had been tainted with strong, painful emotions and followed by equally strong feelings of relief. It was 20 years ago, in a small, Catholic maternity ward in Nairobi, Kenya, when I was in labor with my son Yann. My first child's delivery was away from friends and family because I had to leave Burundi temporarily due to war-related attacks that were happening even in hospitals. I had no Lamaze classes or words of wisdom from elder female relatives to prepare me for an agony that seemed eternal. No pain killers or epidural injections to appease the pain. Just raw, physical suffering.

I was expected to know what to do when in labor. My impression was that the few midwives on duty that day would only tend to the women who were dilated enough to assist them as they released their baby. Until that moment, women were left to themselves with their pain, pleadings, and prayers. From behind the curtains that separated the beds, I could hear women praying aloud in different languages and others screaming for help. Despite all the noise surrounding me, I felt all alone. Alone and frightened. I held dearly to my rosary with one hand as the Virgin Mary appeared to be my only hope to survive the experience of an almost unassisted childbirth. The other hand was holding desperately on the cold metal frame of the headboard to maintain some level of control on the only thing that seemed unchanging and predictable.

I did possess a comforting knowledge that when it was time, the baby would come out. Naturally. Magically almost. At least that was my silent prayer. When the pain became truly unbearable, to the point I hardly knew where I was, who I was, or what I was doing or saying, a couple of midwives and a doctor were standing next to me, and I was witnessing the birth of my beloved son. I will spare you more details, but all I will say is that the instant my son cried, all the pain vanished. Even though the pain that preceded my baby's transition into this world was extreme, the moment he exited, I felt very relieved. Truly liberated.

This memory helped me to begin to put my current pain in perspective. I went back to my former office to gather my personal belongings. As I was packing and maintaining a conversation with my supervisor, it appeared that she seemed to care about whether I was going to be okay. It was raining outside, and I would stop what I was doing from time to time to contemplate the beauty of nature, sympathizing and crying with me.

My supervisor left me alone for short periods of time to get more boxes and other packing material. I took advantage of those moments to close my eyes for a quick prayer, a deep breath, or just to

LOSING MY JOB AND FINDING MYSELF

stand by the window and stare at the rain. Many memories were formed in this office during the short period of time I had occupied it. This space had been my little sanctuary since we had moved into the new building almost four months prior. This space had seen the best and the worse of me, from my most creative moment to my most vulnerable time.

The days following my dismissal were very hard and emotional. I couldn't believe how much it was affecting me. In the big scheme of things, looking at what else I had overcome, this was a joke. But the rejection wasn't new. Old, unresolved feelings around being rejected resurfaced. For two days, I lived in my white robe 24/7. I didn't know how to break the news to my family. My husband thought I was taking "mental health" time off work, but on the third day, he forced me to say something. I told him, matter-of-factly, that I had been fired. He thought I was joking. I took him in the garage, opened the trunk of my Jeep . . . the boxes with our large wedding photo sticking out of them, my African baskets, my mini fridge, and other personal belongs had been there for three days.

He looked at me with so much empathy. He knew how much I had given to that job and to be discharged the way I was pained him truly. He held me in a long and emotional embrace, as I allowed myself to discharge through tears.

As much as I had loved my job, my overall life was out of alignment. My personal and family needs had been put on the back burner. As I started to focus on what was going well for me despite the hurt, I started noticing that, for the first time in a very long time, I finally had *time,* a commodity that had become so scarce in my life, as a result of the demands of my job. From there, I began to see that all the things I had wanted to do, all accomplishments that only existed

TURNING POINTS

in my dreams, could really start manifesting. My focus started to slowly shift to the positive outcomes of an unfortunate situation.

Before long, I decided to spend most of my days writing the book I always knew I had in me. The process was so healing that I would write for hours and hours and even forget to do anything else. I would be up until two in the morning, writing, because it felt so great and I simply couldn't stop. As my book progressed, I also started my consulting business. Former colleagues and partners would contact me and offer me short contracts, thus organically helping me discover my niche and build my enterprise. I also devoted more time to my family as well as the community. I started feeling fulfilled and really pleased with the direction my life was taking. I reached for emotional support from my friends and family and, over time, I filed the hurt and humiliation I experienced away as one more thing I could overcome, even if it took more thought processing to do it. I found a way to forgive those who created that hurt and to thank them for the learning experience it provided for me.

Today, I get to choose what kind of assignments I will take, decide the volume of my work, and establish my own priorities. I can travel and explore the world with my laptop and still be productive. I can be more present in my children's lives and education. I can be there for my husband. I am more in control of my professional world than ever before, which positively impacts everything else I do. I think about the legacy I want to leave behind and try to be mindful of the energy and the actions I embrace daily. Do my choices enable or disable my overall life goals and my legacy? That's the question I ask myself each day, as I go through my life with love, laughter, gratitude, hope, and hard work.

Laetitia Mizero Hellerud

CONCLUSION

Some life experiences are less painful and more purposeful when shared with others. As the empathetic listener takes in the shared story, there is no doubt the teller feels a little bit better, at the very least in that moment. There is healing in the expression of painful experiences and in being heard.

Deciding to share one's story of overcoming adversity can be powerful in many ways. For one, it can help the person extract themselves from the state of victimhood, see their own worth and values, as well as define their priorities to hopefully move on. For the second, unmasking the unspoken truth can help someone else as they start to understand that it is possible to tame, even gain mastery over whatever challenges they are facing.

The stories featured in this book are an illustration of how good things can come from terrible pain or truly horrific life experiences. One of the many lessons to draw from these accounts of past events in the narrators' lives is that when you go through doubts, hurdles, struggles, and suffering, no matter how small or how severe, you need to keep fighting and to not completely despair.

TURNING POINTS

You may either feel paralyzed and stuck or you may naturally want to emotionally react to address the situation or situations. However, *reacting* is not helpful in most cases. *Responding* to the set of circumstances or the state of affairs is vital, but this means finding a balanced approach, using both the brain and the heart to change the trajectory in order to get different outcomes. You will have to find the formula that works best for you. However, you may find inspiration in the lessons shared by the authors of these stories, relating to their own turning points.

According to Dr. Gregg Ury, "A Jewish belief tells us that we are here to join God in repairing the world. Through finding our part in this quest, we complete our life's work and are renewed. Freedom comes when we let go of the ups and downs of our own personal journey and discover the joy and peace of being part of a larger purpose."

The difference between people who have found ways to recover from highly adverse conditions and those who have not is that the former are able to develop a sense of general well-being or inner peace. Resilient individuals do, indeed, understand that they are *not* what happened to them, but what they choose to be, to echo the words of the Swiss psychiatrist and psychoanalyst Carl Gustav Jung. They also understand that blaming has to eventually end in order for them to restore themselves and start living a fulfilling life. They foster a certain level of accountability, enroll help—professional help, more often than not—and power through the suffering to get to the other side of it. When the fear of the painful status quo becomes greater than the fear of the future or the unknown, that's when transformation can truly begin.

The challenge when someone is at this critical point is to make sure the situation doesn't spiral out of control, but rather find a way to

CONCLUSION

deal with it first and then let it become an opportunity to adjust sail and forge ahead. It might also help to look for tools from unconventional sources or try nontraditional techniques. Maybe you can learn from other cultures and how they deal with challenges or tame suffering.

As in the stories featured, many great outcomes came from the most trying situations, although it took years to see that, for some. Some people were also able to make their comeback even greater than their setbacks. We can learn from the wisdom they gathered from their life experiences and shared in the following universal messages.

TAKEAWAY MESSAGES

Read these universal messages to help you find a way through your own adversity.

When an event challenges your life, delay your judgment about what your potential might be until you find a new "normal." The shock of losing your previous "normal" can blind you to possibilities. We are all capable of finding hope, even when it's hard to see through the debris.

Look for a silver lining in your life's misfortunes. There is a hopeful side to even the worst situations, no matter how gloomy it might look from the surface.

You are not alone. In your suffering, God is always with you, even when you don't see how. It can be easy to feel you are the only one going through tunnels of despair or loss, but if you lift your head long

TURNING POINTS

enough to reach out to others—and I mean really reach out—you will be surprised at how many kindred spirits have been there all along.

People are brought into our lives to teach us. Overcoming the challenges they may bring can show you your strength.

You are *not* what happened to you. Your reaction and response to challenges define who you are.

Asking for help can be a sign of strength rather than a sign of weakness.

Human beings are fragile. We are also capable of great resilience.

Your limitations, physical or otherwise, do not define you. You are not the stereotypes society may choose to impose on you.

When you have a decision to make, don't let your ego stand in the way of your happiness. Life is too precious to waste just because you want to protect a false sense of self-importance.

TAKEAWAY MESSAGES

Grieving the loss of something important in your life is necessary. In this process, allow yourself to feel every single emotion. Don't suppress any.

Tomorrow is never guaranteed. Be grateful you are alive.

Happily ever after does not exist. Embrace the trials so you can enjoy the future.

Be open to reinterpreting what you think you know to be true.

Be careful not to apply what you learned as "normal" in your childhood to others. Their experience may have been very different.

Look for the things we all have in common; look beyond what you see. We are more the same than we are different.

THE WAY IT IS
by William Stafford

William Stafford's journey with words began most mornings before sunrise. This simple poem was written 26 days before he passed. The day before, he wrote "Haycutters" and four days later on August 6, 1993, he wrote "November" in honor of Hiroshima Day.

One of his students, the poet Naomi Shihab Nye, wrote, "In our time there has been no poet who revived human hearts and spirits more convincingly than William Stafford. There has been no one who gave more courage to a journey with words, and silence, and an awakened life."

The Way It Is

There's a thread you follow. It goes among
things that change. But it doesn't change.
People wonder about what you are pursuing.
You have to explain about the thread.
But it is hard for others to see.
While you hold it you can't get lost.
Tragedies happen; people get hurt
or die; and you suffer and get old.
Nothing you do can stop time's unfolding.
You don't ever let go of the thread.

—William Stafford, from *The Way It Is:*
New & Selected Poems (Graywolf Press, revised edition, 1999)

ACKNOWLEDGMENTS

This book is the result of a collaborative effort. I was amazed at the number of people who responded positively to my request for turning point stories when I decided to embark on this venture.

I am remarkably grateful for the candor of each and all the contributors as they shared their life experiences with me. They trusted me to work with their stories and to handle them with the utmost respect and dignity.

I offer sincere appreciation to the authors whose stories did not make the final selection. Your stories do matter. Not including them in this particular book was due to reasons beyond the authenticity, the quality, and the content of your narratives.

This project would not have been possible without the contribution from my co-authors whose stories are featured, in no particular order: Keith and Sherry Bjornson; Sarah Dixon-Hackey; Dr. A.M.; Judy Siegle; Lesley Barry; C.M., Ph.D; Vicki Vogel Schmidt; Martina W.H.; Dr. M.J.L.; Brandi Nicole Jude; Unstoppable Tracy Schmitt; B.S.G.; Rebel Marie; and Kerry Ann Leno.

TURNING POINTS

It's also my pleasure to offer thanks to the very talented Jennifer Regner for her expertise in editing and proofreading these stories, Denise Pinkney for her technical support, and Maryanna Young for her overall guidance.

My heartfelt appreciation to beloved friends and family members for being my tireless cheerleaders, especially when I am self-doubting or going through life's hardships. Fond thoughts to my Re-evaluation Counseling community, which includes at this point Deb White, Joel Friesz, Yann Niteka, Rachel Asleson, Bruce Mizero, Cyusa Alexandre Ntwali, and our well-cultured, much-loved teacher and leader Claudia Murphy.

I hold in high regard all my educators, colleagues, spiritual leaders, mentors, and all my "life teachers." Thank you for impacting my growth by molding my spirit and challenging my intellect.

Words cannot describe the level of indebtedness to my treasured and loving husband Mark for being the quiet enabler behind everything I have accomplished since leaving steady income streams. He works hard and sacrifices a lot so that our children, Yann and Nicole, as well as myself, can pursue our passions. My hope is that we all make him proud.

Last, but certainly not least, to anyone who assisted directly or indirectly to making this book a reality, as well as the innumerable patrons who support my work, I am wholeheartedly thankful.

ABOUT THE AUTHOR

A native of tropical but politically unstable Burundi, Laetitia Mizero Hellerud immigrated to the United States of America as a refugee. She uses her life and work experiences to make connections with others, no matter where they come from.

Laetitia is passionate about integrating communities and global human rights. Part of her work includes empowering immigrants and mainstream communities to build on each one's strengths, pulling from their cultural commonalities and differences.

Her wide array of services ranges from coaching and mentoring individual leaders to assisting corporations, educational entities, and other organized groups with their intercultural competence development, as well as overall inclusion needs, through a process that includes assessments and goal-planning.

Laetitia is educated both in Burundi and the U.S. She has lived and traveled extensively in several countries in Africa, North America, and Europe. She is fluent in multiple languages.

She considers herself a seeker, a learner, and a social justice and human rights activist. She is also a keynote speaker, a connector, an educator, and an optimizer.

TURNING POINTS

Laetitia and her husband, Mark, who is a retired farmer and an attorney, live and work both in North Dakota and in Minnesota. Their blended family includes two adult children, Yann and Nicole, and a springer spaniel, Laurel.

UBUNTU Consulting

ABOUT UBUNTU CONSULTING

Laetitia Mizero Hellerud founded UBUNTU Consulting to provide educational services by developing, facilitating, coaching, and delivering customized workshops and seminars that support the growth of individuals, teams, and organizations within their own vision. UBUNTU Consulting's areas of expertise include cultural competence, cross-cultural leadership, inclusion, equity, and related fields.

Laetitia administers IDI® (Intercultural Development Inventory) assessments, profiles, and development goals and plans for individuals, as well as groups and organizations. She also provides customized expertise to create welcoming and integrated communities.

ABOUT *BEING AT HOME IN THE WORLD*

We all make decisions about the direction our lives will take based on our circumstances and embrace the leadership demands our lives place on us. We all share a vision of leading a life in safety and creating a better life for those we love.

As a four-time refugee, change and adaptation has become a way of life for Laetitia Mizero Hellerud. Having to adapt to this way of thinking since childhood, she learned to rely on her own decisions and, at the same time, accept the love and help of others to survive. In *Being at Home in the World*, Laetitia shares what she has learned about adaptation—about finding your home—in the midst of chaos and struggle. It starts with an open mind and an open heart.